So This Is College

So This Is College

PAUL H. LANDIS

State Professor of Rural Sociology
The State College of Washington

McGRAW-HILL BOOK COMPANY, INC.

1954   NEW YORK   TORONTO   LONDON

Preface

In our time youth are offered many guides, yet I am convinced that they have never been so self-sufficient and so capable of self-direction as now. Moral maturity comes early in our culture, for the adolescent suddenly becomes a member of the teen-age group, which in our culture is a group apart from adult society—independent, wise, and self-determining in its own way. This group of young people make choices for themselves their ancestors were never expected to make even in adulthood, for the ancestors always moved in the protective environs of adult opinion.

A social climate of freedom—of unchaperoned pair association and early marriage, of vocational choice in a world of many occupations, of social climbing that far more often than not takes the child into a world for which the experience of the parental home gave no preparation, of social mobility that very early takes him beyond the restraining environs of the neighborhood, of a moral system that is a patchwork of many patterns—demands of youth choices and adjustments. College young people are at the focal point of this often painful transition to adulthood. Problems for many are often so numerous that no guide can more than touch isolated bits of their experience.

I am not an oracle for the new generation. No adult can be. From twenty-five years' experience on college campuses I have gained insight. I depend on this in part, but even more on excerpts from student autobiographies in which young people describe their own characteristic struggles.

I am happy to acknowledge the help of Miss Barbara Ruth Day, who, as a Master's Degree project, selected from my gleaning of more than a thousand autobiographies 238 that best represent typical crises and adjustments, and tabulated and described these experiences; to Mrs. Joanne Haer, former student counselor at The State College of Washington for her help and insight in interpreting parts of these materials; and to my son Vincent, now a graduate student at the University of Minnesota, for criticism and help on the manuscript.

Paul H. Landis

Contents

CHAPTER I

This Road Has Been Traveled Before

There are many times in life when it is a great comfort to know that one is on a well-traveled path—that no matter how difficult the climb, many others have made it before us—that they have shared the same feelings of anxiety and hope, discouragement and elation.

Why this book was written

In teaching introductory sociology in three different colleges and universities, at the end of the course I have always required a term paper in which students are asked to analyze the development of their personalities, employing the sociological and psychological concepts learned in the course.

To assure honesty I promise that no one else will read their papers for four years. This is to allow time for them and their friends to graduate. Each student is asked to put his name on the upper right-hand corner of the first sheet of paper only, and I promise to clip it off as soon as the term paper is graded. After four years these papers are added to my collection, which any student may read.

At first many students object to writing an autobiography, but after it is done, almost all of them feel that they gained a great deal from the experience. It relieves them to take their complexes and problems out and look them over. For the first time many of them try to find meaning in the various experiences that caused them suffering during their teen years, some of which cause them trouble still. Many have found this experience helpful, too, in solving their own problems.

Reading more than a thousand such papers has led me to think that a book focused upon the common problems and adjustments these autobiographies reveal could be helpful to the younger college student and perhaps to a lesser extent to all teen-agers.

The reason we are so often overwhelmed by our problems is that we think no one else has them. I hope those who read this book will see in the cases presented here enough experiences and problems typical of their own strivings to feel that they are not alone. To know that the road has been traveled before and that its dangers have been surmounted always brings comfort and a feeling of safety to us at any stage in life.

Moreover, the next best thing to sharing one's problems with someone else is to read the problems of others, finding relief for himself in the experiences of others.

Thinking that many young people who read this will be looking ahead to their college days or will already be starting them, I have begun with Lorraine's account of her first days in college—what she felt as well as what she did. Likely as not, you will soon be writing such a theme as part of an English I assignment.

Lorraine's first days in college

Complete with the new "dress" clothes, radio, clock, and other paraphernalia recommended by the little orientation booklet I had received, I was eager to start on my new adventure—college.

Having grown up in a small town, I had been "in" with the girls, boys, parents, and teachers and was a leader in school and outside activities. I had no more to worry about than a summer job, a new dress, and an occasional "breaking up" with boy friends. With this background I set off for college and the big wide world.

I'm afraid my high-school experience with living was not quite adequate for the problems I encountered in college.

I had three roommates of various shapes, sizes, personalities, and of widely varied backgrounds. One was a farm girl, another a preacher's daughter, and the third a missionary's daughter from Puerto Rico.

My distinctive "green freshman" appearance highly noticeable, I stood in line for registration for hours and filled out endless numbers of cards (on both sides).

Then I stood in another line to see my faculty adviser who promptly crossed out half my schedule because the sections were filled or I had signed up for upper-division course by mistake. After rearranging everything to the adviser's satisfaction, I was herded by helpful service-organization members to the line waiting to pay fees and from there all the way across campus to the bookstore where I was welcomed into another line.

Through all these lines the strange new language of college life was noticeable. "Did you get BA 29 at 10:00?"

"When are your floats?" "Did you get Dr. Blizblah for psych? I hear he's O.K. Easy grader, too." "Have you seen the new Kappa Sig house? I wonder how many pledges they are taking."

On and on it went. A world of strange faces, stranger names, and endless topics of conversation.

Then rushing began. My past knowledge of Greek life consisted of knowing girls belonged in sororities and boys in fraternities. The names of the Greek houses were a mystery, as I couldn't tell which were for girls and which for boys.

After asking numerous questions of a few upperclassmen in the dorm, I decided to "rush." I still had very vague ideas of the reasons for sororities. But I read the rushing schedule and found I was supposed to dress in suit, hat, gloves, and heels and be at the Student Union building at a specified time. From there I would start out for an afternoon of what was called "open house" tours.

I was there at the appointed time. Most of the freshman rushees looked as bewildered and scared as I felt. Except for a few who seemed to know *all about it* and voiced their knowledge, the rest of us were nervously quiet, wondering just what was going to happen.

Then a dozen cars drove up, driven by sorority members who were to take us to various houses where the groups were to entertain us. It was at this moment that my first real feeling of "social inferiority" cropped up. The sorority girls all looked beautiful. They were immaculately dressed in clothes of the highest fashion, or so it seemed to me. They were so poised and at ease with us!

Overwhelming doubt possessed me. I look like a wreck! Why didn't I buy a suit like that? Gee, I wish I had a better figure. And why am I so near-sighted that I have to wear these horrible glasses? I just know my stocking seams are crooked. Guess I'd better take my glasses off, even if I can't see. I look so much better without them. Oh, there's a spot on one of my gloves. I'd better carry it so they won't notice.

I never had felt so self-conscious, awkward, and embarrassed in my life.

We climbed into the cars and made polite conversation for the duration of the ride.

I was nervous and I was scared. We stopped in front of a house that looked to me like a small mansion.

Swarms of girls awaited us at the door. They were all dressed in frothy formals of pastel colors and looked and acted as though they had stepped out of *Vogue*. They seemed to ooze personality, poise, and self-confidence.

We were given name cards and introduced through a reception line of house officers and alums. After this seemingly long ordeal we were seated in small groups with three or four of the sorority girls. Everyone seemed to have something to talk about but me. They all knew some of the same people, or places, and conversation flowed about me.

While trying to concentrate on the conversation, laugh, or comment at appropriate times, I was silently tearing myself down in every respect and feeling more dejected and inadequate every minute.

By the time we reached the last house that afternoon I was miserable, dead tired, and ready to call it quits with rushing.

But rushing continued and I continued with it, mostly because I learned by talking to the other freshmen that most had shared some of my feelings. We all adopted a "we really don't care" attitude as the week progressed. We had heard about and seen how heartbreaking being dropped can be to some of the girls who really cared to belong.

Surprisingly, I was pledged to the house I liked the best. I still sometimes wonder how it happened.

School began—with it came the responsibility of seeing myself off to eight o'clock classes with no mother calling to me a dozen times to "hurry or you'll be late to school." There were house rules, signing out wherever I went, and new hours to keep.

Classes, too, were strange. I wandered around campus with my schedule book and map open, hunting for a building with a name coinciding with the one listed beside my course. It seemed funny not to sit at a desk, and in class to have to take volumes of notes from a seemingly "untouchable" man who walked into the room when the bell rang, talked for an hour and left, leaving behind a huge assignment due the next hour of that class.

It wasn't much like high-school days to sit down and spend three or four hours a day with various textbooks, either.

But everyone else was doing it, too. I had started my college career.

Self and others

Lorraine's feelings—a mixture of joy and apprehension —were no more unusual than were her experiences as a green freshman. Most students admit having felt self-conscious, awkward, uninteresting, even disillusioned and fearful during the first days of their college life.

Yes, every young person meets these common adjustments upon entering college. But whether he emerges from the ordeal a stronger, more confident student or a beaten man depends a great deal upon how he has learned to see himself and what his general attitudes are toward other people.

We know a lot about Lorraine, for example, by considering her feelings of inferiority and awkwardness, her curiosity, her good humor and "stick-to-itiveness." We can know more about ourselves, as well, by examining our attitudes toward ourselves and toward others.

As a matter of fact, we cannot begin to know ourself until we know how we stand with others. The little scheme below, though oversimplified somewhat, tells of this relationship very briefly. In fact, it shows how our treatment by others through the years since our birth makes our inner self react in the peculiar manner it does. Here is the outline:

To understand any person, including ourselves, know his attitudes toward himself and toward others.

I. Attitudes toward self fall into two contrasting types:
   1. Individual A feels sure of himself, is emotionally secure, senses a unity within himself (is integrated).
   2. Individual B feels unsure of himself, is emotionally anxious, often has an unprovoked sense of guilt, senses strain and tension within himself (lacks integration).
II. Attitudes toward others also fall into two contrasting types:
   1. Individual A is friendly and sociable, is in harmony with his social groups (is adjusted).
   2. Individual B is hostile and aggressive, or retires within

himself to escape as many social contacts as possible. He may be belligerent and hostile or overly submissive and docile. He feels out of harmony with his social group (is maladjusted).

By the time we reach college, we are generally a blend of these two sets of attitudes toward self and others. Some approach the unadjusted extreme; others the adjusted extreme. Where we fall depends on the way the groups with which we have associated have treated us since the day we were born. If we have been loved and accepted by parents and brothers and sisters, have had close and intimate friends, the chances are that we tend to be like individual A, both in attitudes toward self and toward others. If, on the other hand, we have lacked such consideration by others, we are likely to approach type B in both attitudes.

What we are in both self and other attitudes depends then on the kind of associations we have had with others up to now.

If we have some or many of the traits of individual B in the outline, college is our big chance to turn over a new leaf—to try to build relationships with others in our new group that will make us feel more secure in all our other relationships. For many of us, college is our first time away from home and away from the old gang with whom we've grown up since earliest childhood. Here at last, among strangers, is the opportunity we need to become a new and better person.

CHAPTER II

A Personal Inventory

To live is to have problems

Every person has his problems. We are not unique because we have them; in fact, we would be downright odd without them. The sooner we reconcile ourselves to the fact that we shall be solving problems the rest of our lives, the more successful we shall be in our adjustments and the more realistic and mature our outlook will be.

Our problems are never quite the same at any two stages in life. A four-year-old will argue with his parents, "I got to have a tricycle 'cause my legs get tired walkin' to all the places I got to go." In six or eight years he is just as insistent on his need for a new bike. By sixteen or so, some kind of jalopy will be an absolute must. So we face new issues as we go through different phases of our life cycle. Problems of marriage will differ from those of our single years; those of middle life from our earlier years; and those of old age from middle life.

So the cycle of life carries us along over the same old path that our parents traveled, and all human beings before us. The scenery along the path of life changes considerably from generation to generation, but man and his everyday problems in living remain very much the same.

Our college days are no exception. Many of the problems we meet are completely new to us—far different from those we knew in high school. But the problems in themselves are not new. They have been worrying young men and women like us in colleges all over the country for many years. As a result, it is possible to predict fairly closely just what kinds of problems will be disturbing the freshmen on any campus now and in the future.

A student of mine, Barbara Ruth Day, in work on her master's degree, tabulated the problems mentioned by 238 students in their autobiographies in my collection. Here in order are the ones mentioned most frequently:

1. An inferiority complex
2. Compensating for inferiority feelings
3. Daydreaming
4. Disillusionment in shifting from the small local group to the larger group
5. Sex problems
6. Feelings of insecurity
7. Undesirable traits of temperament
8. Introversion
9. Religious problems
10. Death in family
11. Fear
12. Emancipating myself from home
13. Disillusionment with friends and adults
14. Economic problems
15. Family conflicts
16. Delinquency
17. Sensitiveness

18. Homesickness
19. Parents forcing their wishes or ambitions on me
20. My inability to take responsibility and make decisions
21. Conflict between previous and new attitudes and beliefs
22. Rivalry with brothers and sisters
23. Not being accepted by a fraternity or sorority
24. Divorce of parents
25. Foster-home problems
26. Shifting from rural area to city living
27. Superiority complex
28. Conflict over college rules and regulations
29. Moral disillusionment
30. Hero or idol worship
31. Revolt against authority

This is a picture of the areas in which young people of college age have had or are having problems. The most typical problems will be covered in the following chapters to see just what form they take and some of the ways in which they can be handled successfully. This will give us an idea of how problems stack up during the years from seventeen to nineteen.

Before going on to a consideration of problems we are likely to meet, let us take a look at what our personalities are now and how they got to be this way.

What are we in personality now?

Flesh and blood. The chemist tells us that the elements in our bodies are worth only a few cents—most of us is water. Personality is, of course, more than water, salt, proteins, and the other substances that make up our bodies.

First of all, life is added. There is a lot of difference in the value of a dead body and a live one. All insurance companies recognize this fact.

Personality is in part a matter of how much life we have. The vivacious, energetic person has more to offer society than the slow, plodding one. We rate the person with lots of vitality at the top in personality when we are considering the physical part of personality alone.

Mind. We are also made up of mind. Without it we are of no usefulness to society—have no ability to talk with others or to live and play with them. Bright minds are worth more than dull minds. In most situations we give the bright mind first place in rank when we are rating people according to mental ability.

Emotion. Personality is also emotion, for every human being is an engine filled with drives that make him want to act and do. A person loves and hates, wants and rejects. He is capable of many emotions, some of which draw people to him, others of which drive them away. Those who are most capable of love and kindness, goodness and mercy, are generally rated more highly than those given to hate and jealousy, bullying and pride.

These are the things of which personality is made up, and yet it is more than all of them put together. We are each a combination of body, mind, and emotion which has been built in a slightly different environment. We carry along in our bodies, minds, and emotions the residue of our past experiences. They are a part of the way we act today.

Experience. No one could possibly know how we are going to act in a given situation without knowing a great deal about the experiences that have shaped us as we have grown up.

Here, an example may help. Most people like lemon pie, and the hostesses who serve it usually do so with pride and the certainty of popularity. I do not like lemon pie. It almost turns my stomach upside down even to write about it. If you were writing about it, probably your mouth would water. You would be swallowing and unconsciously running your tongue along your lips at the thought of the sweet lemon-flavored custard with the whipped-cream surface and flaky crust underneath. But I shall never want lemon pie again.

It all happened when I was in college. I was waiting on tables to pay my way. Like most boys of my age, I usually left the table after a meal about as hungry as when I sat down. One day there were several pieces of lemon pie left. The cook said to us waiters, "You boys may clean up the pie." I ate only three pieces, but I was so sick afterwards that I haven't been able to face a lemon pie since.

If it were worth the effort, I suppose by taking a little nip of lemon pie now and then, I could learn to eat it again. It would be better yet if this were done in an atmosphere of soft music or congenial companionship.

We are all full of little quirks like this because our personalities have been worked over by experiences we have had through the years since we were born. Some have physical scars or have lost a finger or two. Some have been affected by sickness; others have robust baseball-pitchers' arms. The things we have done and the things that have been done to us have helped to form our bodies and have made them whatever asset or liability they are to our personalities today.

Our minds have become a kind of tool chest in which are stored all sizes and shapes of knowledge of this and that. We began life as ignorant and helpless creatures. Now the tool chest is pretty well furnished with habits that make us act without thinking in accomplishing most of our simple everyday tasks of living.

We have some specialized tools, like arithmetic or a foreign language, that we may use little, but they are nice to have in case we need them. We have stored up the necessary manners and skills that make us move with some comfort and assurance among our fellows.

Some of us have learned much by the time we enter the late teens; others relatively little. Whether much or little, it is a part of us. Some think that we never forget anything we learn. That's hard to believe. At least it would take a very high fever to get us to recall many things we are supposed to have learned in arithmetic or algebra.

What our minds have in equipment depends on the associations we have had. We are good with fork and spoon about three times a day but as awkward as infants with chopsticks. We may be good on roller skates but stagger like a drunk on ice skates. Generally speaking, the more mental tools we have, the better we get along in our adjustments with people.

Finally, we come to emotions, which are such a vital part of the way we act as persons. Do we have a turbulent volcano within us, or is all calm and peaceful? This, too, has been determined at least in part by the experiences that came our way as we have grown up.

Will we fight at the drop of a hat, or do we slink away and brood about our hurts? Are we jealous of everyone who is content and successful, or can we feel happy for them and wish them further luck? Are we courageous and hopeful about life, or do we live in anxiety and fear of what we do not know?

Most of us are some combination of all these feelings. We are sometimes up and sometimes down.

Where did we get these feelings and fears that rule us? We got them just as I got my dislike for lemon pie. Somewhere along the line we had a bitter experience and haven't been able to forget it.

We may have forgotten consciously and not know when it happened or even what happened, but our emotions have not forgotten. They were pained, and the pain lingers on to warn us of new danger.

Painful emotions are nature's automatic warning signals to tell us of danger. But emotions are not always sensible. In fact, they never are determined by reason. They are automatic and work without our commanding them to do so.

Fortunately for us, emotions are not all of an unpleasant type. We also have a kind of hope chest full of pleasant emotions. It is made up of memories of those who have loved us and have been kind. It is stored with the happy feelings that came when we had good times with friends and family. It is full of little hopes that tell us these good times will come again in the future.

In it are dreams of what we can have, of what we shall be, and of the good we shall do tomorrow.

This hope chest has been filled in part by our successes and the joy they brought. These emotions are like good music, making us forget the painful emotions and experiences that would make us as shy of life as a skittish colt.

But what has all this got to do with you and college, you may wonder. After all, the experiences that made you what you are now are things of the past, and pleasant or otherwise, nothing can change them.

As a matter of fact, your happiness and success in college will depend a good deal on just how well you know yourself and how you got to be the way you are.

Testing ourselves

Maybe it is time to take stock of ourselves and try to learn just where the sore spots, and the bright spots, are in our personalities. It can be a painful experience, but it can also be useful. Let's try a little test.

Take a sheet of paper and try to answer each of these questions. Some of the answers may make you blush, but no one else need see them. This is simply a test for facing ourselves. Some of the answers may be silly and nonsensical, but write them down anyway.

I hate ——
I wish ——
I fear ——

I hope ——
I love ——
I'm embarrassed when ——
The thing I'm most afraid of is ——
I want most to be ——
The thing that bothers me most is ——
Regarding myself, I feel ——
The person who worries me most is ——
I'm most cheerful when ——
I'm deeply happy when ——
My greatest interest in life is ——
The person who means most to me is ——
The ones who love me most are ——
I like most in leisure time to ——
I have great respect for ——
My health is——
My ability is ——

Studying our answers

Your hate. Study these answers now and try to see if you
can understand why you react as you do. From what experiences is your hate derived? Is it against persons, things, or
ideas? Is it individual, family, or political in origin? Does
it make sense? Has the object of your hate really earned
it? What peculiarities of behavior, what deviations and
quirks result from it? Do you need help from a counselor
or will time bring its own cure?

Some of us will list one of our parents in answering the
question, "I hate," if we answer honestly. This may shock
us and make us feel that we have done an unpardonable
thing. No harm is done. It is a good thing to take our hates

out and have a look at them. If we have answered that way, why? Have our parents denied us something that we wanted very much? Would we have answered the same way last week? Last year? Tomorrow?

Perhaps we listed them both under "I love" and "I hate."

All of us have what the psychologist calls "ambivalent" attitudes toward those who are very close to us. This means a combination of love and hatred. We often fluctuate from one to the other.

Often during the years of adolescence, when we are trying to free ourselves from our parents' domination, we resent their love and attention, temporarily hate them because they know us so well and have made us so dependent on them. This is a natural revolt, and the hatred wears off as we get more freedom and maturity.

Some revolt of this kind against the very close attachments of childhood must come if we are to grow up. Here is the reaction of a girl who still worries about the break she made with her parents near the end of her freshman year in college:

"Just one big happy family," or so my parents think. They like to tell people about how everyone in our family just can't do without one another. We do everything as a group—picnics, movies, parties, and so on. Both Mom and Dad would be heartbroken if one of us suggested we would rather be among people of our own age. Dad even arranged for his own transfer so my brother and I wouldn't have to go away from home to attend college.

But things aren't as perfect as they appear on the surface. While we appreciate their love and years of care, both my brother and I resent the tight hold Mom and Dad have on our lives. Tom, my brother, once said, "If I were drafted, Mom would probably insist on moving the entire family into my barracks." He said it to be nasty, but Mom thought it was a compliment to her motherly love.

Personally, I've decided to put an end to this unbearable situation while I can still love and respect my parents. Next fall I'm going to announce that I am leaving for the State U, and that I don't want them to try to arrange another transfer.

Does this sound terrible? It makes me feel guilty to say these things, but they are true; and I know I will soon grow to hate my parents if I do not have some freedom and young companionship.

Your wish. Is it realistic and possible of attainment? Does it tell anything about the important things of life you may have missed—affection, security, or exciting new experiences? Is it worthy of your striving, or is it time to cast it away as a thing of childhood and immaturity?

Notice the differences, for example, between the wishes of these two college freshmen:

"What do I wish for most? Oh, brother! I could fill a notebook on this subject, but it could all be boiled down to four cashmere sweaters and a drawer full of argyle socks. Clothes make the man on this campus; without the right rags you just don't rate."

"My wish? Simple . . . a pet. More than anything else in the world I'd like to have the complete love and undivided loyalty of something. I'd like a dog, for example, that would follow me around and never bother with anyone else, or a horse that wouldn't let anyone else ride him but me. This sounds rather childish for an eighteen-year-old, but it is the way I feel."

Your love. Is it a thing, person, or divine being? Is love the core of your life, the force that has given it meaning? Is the object of your love worthy of your devotion? If love of people is your dominant emotion, the chances are that you are a happy, well-adjusted person. Hate and hostilities make us unhappy. Love of material things above people may also deprive us of happiness and good social adjustment. Christ spoke a profound truth when He said it is easier for a camel to pass through the needle's eye than for a rich man to enter the kingdom of heaven. Love of material things above the love of our fellowmen makes social adjustment very hard. Miserly souls are always selling life short.

Go through each of your answers and see what you can learn about the values and interests of your life.

It may be the answers we hardly dared to write down that are most significant in understanding our deepest problems. Maybe we actually dared not write down some answer. Is it because we are afraid to face it? Is it that it deals with an issue about which we can do nothing? Or is it merely an issue we have avoided, knowing all the time we should come to terms with it?

Analyzing where the quirks in our personality came from. As you look over this list, try to think where you got the feelings and attitudes you have. In some cases, you will be able to trace them back to some happy or unhappy experience. In other cases, you may not be able to explain them at all. The experience that produced them has long been forgotten by our minds, even though it lingers on in our emotions.

It may not be a direct experience that caused this emotion. Sometimes our emotions associate one object with another until we are not sure of the origin at all.

A psychologist named John B. Watson once studied fears in young children. He found that small children are afraid of loud noises. But he could soon make them afraid of many other things by associating a loud noise with other objects, persons, or things. For example, the small baby, if touched with a furry object like a hand muff at the same time that a loud noise was made, was soon frightened by any furry object, even a woman wearing a fur coat.

Many of our fears and other warning emotions make no sense at all, but they came to us through some experience that makes our autonomic nervous system act as though they did.

Mary, in her autobiography, says:

> I have four pet fears: steep, narrow attic stairs; bears; poorly built swimming rafts; and confined spaces. I recall the incidents which caused the first three, but I can give no explanation for the last one. All memory of incidents that may have caused it has been lost.

It is a good thing to study our emotions and to see if, after all, they do make sense. If they don't and they are damaging to us, it is time to begin to associate pleasant experiences with them and see if we can change our automatic reactions.

If we have been told ghost stories that scared us half to death as children, we may still be afraid to be alone in the dark. That doesn't make sense, and it is terribly awkward to go through life being afraid of the dark. By playing soft music alone in the darkness or having other such pleasant experiences, we can frequently succeed in reconditioning ourselves and in losing our fears.

Our groundless fears, our hates, our complexes and jealousies are always barriers to happy, successful living. But during our college years they become particularly difficult problems. The constant demands of classes and outside activities require cool heads, happy hearts, and all the self-confidence we can muster.

CHAPTER III

Am I Man or Mouse?

Inferiority feelings

A rural neighbor used to say, when he felt down in the dumps, "I'm feelin' lower'n a snake's hips."

That's pretty low! But after those first few days of college during which they are questioned, counseled, examined, advised, and admonished to do thus and so, most freshmen have long since begun to feel pretty low-down and insignificant.

If there is anything we all want to be, it is someone of importance. It isn't that we always want to be the center of attention; we just don't want to feel completely left out and ignored. One of the strongest wishes we possess is to be accepted and respected by our fellows.

Most of us felt we were somebody in the home town and high school from which we came. Now all of a sudden we are without a place in the new scheme of things. All the old inferiorities which plagued most of us in early adolescence are likely to crop up, and a few new ones with them. At least this is a common experience. If you haven't had it, you are lucky.

If we can see how they developed, it may help us to get

at the roots of some of these feelings of inferiority. And, lest we add new inferiorities to the old, it is time we began to consider seriously how to make our place in the sun, so that we will not feel completely overshadowed by those who seem to push their way into the limelight in every circumstance.

How inferiority feelings originate

Our feelings of inferiority—and few human beings are without them—originate in failure and in fear of failure. Everyone wants to show up well, but in many situations during childhood and on through the early teens, we have blundered and fallen short of our own expectations as well as those of others. These failures make sore spots in our personality—spots that bring us pain whenever we think of them.

The amount of pain associated with our failures is due to (1) the seriousness of the failure, (2) the amount of respect it cost us among our fellows, and (3) the sensitiveness of our temperament. Some of us suffer much over little shortcomings; others suffer little over even major ones. The famous psychologist William James divided people into two types: the "tough minded" and the "tender minded."

Those who suffer much over their personal failures or imagined failures are said to have an "inferiority complex," that is, a set of emotionally charged ideas centering about failure. Such a complex may become so touchy that any reminder of it by others, or by some new experience in which we fear failure, completely upsets us. We tighten up and get awkward, or embarrassed and literally scared of our own shadow.

At its worst, an inferiority complex may defy all logic. Karl Menninger, a psychiatrist, tells about a college student who came to him completely whipped. Herman was elected class president, was on the student paper, made good grades, and had many friends. But all this recognition failed to cover over an inferiority complex that had developed during early high school when the boy felt that he had to hide from his schoolmates the fact that his father had had a mental breakdown and was spending a term in a mental hospital. His mother had treated it secretly and kept Herman away from other children. At that time Herman developed such a feeling of inferiority that no amount of later success had been able to make him feel that he was anything but disgraced and inadequate. He felt that he was cheating his schoolmates by not telling them the kind of fellow he really was.

"It doesn't make sense," you say. "Why should a smart young man feel so about such a common thing as mental illness in the family, something he couldn't help in the first place?"

It doesn't make sense from a logical standpoint, but emotions don't need to make sense to overthrow us. Your inferiority feelings probably don't make sense either, but there they are, and you have to live with them. Others would laugh if you mentioned them, and would point out how foolish it is to feel so sensitive about such unimportant things; but if an inferiority complex is ours, we don't laugh it away. The reason we do not is that it is associated

in our emotions with slights and hurts, with embarrass-
ments and humiliations, with blushings and shame. This
is nature's automatic way of warning us against getting
hurt again.

We rarely mention our inferiorities to others, because
we are ashamed to admit that we have such feelings. We
are more self-conscious about them than almost anything
else. If we could talk about them, sort of take them out of
ourselves and look at them, let a friend or two or a counselor look them over with us, they would shrink in size
and begin to vanish. Now is a good time to start, if we
have the courage.

Letting off steam

Emotional complexes locked up within us become like
steam bottled up in a boiler. The tighter it is held the more
pressure it exerts, until something has to burst. If Herman
had talked his feeling of inferiority over with a high-school
counselor or a close friend, it would never have so completely overwhelmed him. They would have helped him
to see how he got the complex and why it really didn't
make sense. He could have shared his feelings with them
and thus relieved his anxiety. From there he could have
taken the first steps toward solving the problem.

Most of us keep our inferiority feelings to ourselves.
Some put on a bold front and act as though they command
the world. Sometimes the more inferior we feel the more
bold we become. Not all are like that. Some who feel inferior approach all situations with great timidity, fearful

lest they repeat some mistake that has caused them to suffer before.

Areas where inferiority develops

A study of student autobiographies shows that there are four main aspects of life in which feelings of inferiority are likely to center.

First, we may suffer from a feeling of physical inadequacy. This usually arises from one of three sources: because we are physically handicapped by a marked deformity; because we feel awkwardly large and ungainly or weak and undersized; or because we lack the necessary skills for competing in athletic events or dancing. Occasionally it is some other shortcoming that makes us feel we are not up to par in body make-up.

Alfred Adler, the psychologist who originated the concept "inferiority complex," believed that all inferiority was "organ inferiority," that is, physical in origin.

I do not believe this is so, but there are many cases in history, as well as in student autobiographies, where organ inferiority was a basic factor in personality development. There was Lord Byron, for example, the sensitive and violent-natured poet, with his clubfoot; Somerset Maugham, master story writer, who reports having suffered inferiority because of certain facial features he considered unattractive to others; Franklin D. Roosevelt, the statesman who was crippled.

We feel inferior about our physical traits only because the people around us tend to treat us as being different.

In our society the fat girl may feel inferior. In parts of South America it is said that the fat woman receives the most proposals. Would she feel inferior there? Hardly!

Here are a few examples of the way young people have reacted to physical handicaps. June writes:

> I was healthy, I was tall, but I was also fat. This never bothered me at home where my family and playmates accepted it.
>
> Then I started to school. It was there I found I couldn't run as fast, jump rope as long, or play baseball like the other kids could. I was usually one of the last ones chosen when they picked out teams for school sports. I became more aware of this as I progressed through grade school and, feeling so left out, I turned more and more to my studies.
>
> The thought of starting high school filled me with dread. I could almost hear the upperclassmen remarking about my size. But I decided to try athletics again and turned out for girl's basketball. Much to my surprise, and because of my height, I became a valuable forward on the team. Even so, it took me a long time to get over the self-consciousness I felt while on the basketball floor.
>
> This same self-consciousness led me to refuse dates in high school with the excuse that I was going to be an "old maid and career woman." I still have not overcome using this rationalization with the fellows.

Sally had an operation on her arm and finally it had to be removed. She writes:

> My whole world was changed. Every single thing I did had to be done differently; people whispered wherever

I went; just when the other girls my age were thrilled with their new interests—dancing and dating—I was treated like a "good scout," but was tactfully barred from these pleasures that most girls live for. I became depressed and embittered. I lay awake nights remembering the days I had spent on ski trips and the ribbons I had won at horse shows. I thought, "What am I living for? What good am I now?"

My parents suffered with me, and waited on me hand and foot. This broke down the self-reliance I had possessed, and I brooded while my family jumped at my beck and call. This went on for months; but fortunately, I had enough good sense to finally get wise to myself. I said to myself, "I'll show them. They can't hold me down." I put my whole personality to work, and decided to conquer nature.

In spite of my parents' objections, I wanted to quit the convent, for my mishap had caused me to lose what little faith I had in religion. They finally consented to my wish, and I entered a public high school as a junior. The change was a drastic one, for no longer were the teachers interested in me personally—I was just one of the mob who had to "do or die." This change was exactly what I needed, for now I had to adjust myself to this new environment, and I had little time for self-pity. I compensated directly for my handicap by adapting myself to my new physical structure and learning to do again everything that I once had done. I learned to manicure my own fingernails, fix my hair, and balance myself on skis and on horseback. My old determination regained, I again won events in horse shows, in spite of my handicap. I was a leader in high school, being rather aggressive and so eager to succeed. Other students admired and respected me.

I never talked about my arm or made excuses for being unable to swim, play cards, or drive a car. I put up a front of self-sufficiency, and I would have been completely successful if girls did not place such an importance on social life. Boys and girls alike enjoyed my company, but boys never asked me to go to dances, and only occasionally was I invited to a party. Some girls are not the type to dance and "gad about," but I had everything it takes, except two arms. I realized this, and it hurt to see less attractive girls talking about and getting ready for dances. I tried to be gay and pretend my life was filled with excitement, but I would occasionally lapse into a bitter mood.

Things are beginning to straighten out. Here at college many of the students are quite mature, and my disability is becoming less and less of a social handicap.

Both June and Sally, once they found outlets for getting recognition within their group, began to overcome their inferiority by compensating successfully. At the time they wrote, there were still a few painful spots in their personalities, centering about their physical differences; but they had made up for them in so many ways that they were actually more interesting and capable persons than they would have been had they not had to fight to find a place for themselves among their fellows.

A second area out of which inferiority feelings grow is that of lack of ability. This is, of course, bound to be painful in school situations. It is most painful when we are overshadowed by someone who is close to us, as was the case with Chuck. He writes:

My brother was three years ahead of me in school and a very brilliant student. My parents, as well as all the teachers, expected me to match his record of good grades. I guess I was well hidden when the brains were passed out. While my brother got A's with very little effort, I slaved for C's. The more I heard about my brilliant brother, the more inadequate I felt. To keep from displaying my feelings, I spent no more time with my family than was absolutely necessary. Instead of staying at home evenings with my brother and sisters, I would go to the homes of my friends where I wasn't constantly hounded by the subject of grades.

When Chuck wrote this account, he was in a college several hundred miles from the one his older brother was attending. He no longer had to live under the shadow of his brother's record and was beginning to feel as though he could be satisfied with achievements of which he was capable.

Somewhere along the way we have to accept and make the most of the abilities we have, yet it is a hard thing to do. Before we get through college we shall know, if we have not guessed it already, that there are many kinds of ability that count as much or more than cracking the examination with an A. If we are going into a profession, some A's may be very important to us, but in most fields a sincere smile, a sense of humor, genuine friendliness, the knack of being helpful to others, and the ability to rise above jealousy will have a value not shown on the grade books.

We need to develop these abilities as much as the ability to score well on an exam.

The third field in which inferiority feelings develop is economic. Lack of money is a hard problem to crack. If we were to get a job and work, it would, of course, be a cinch, but we are determined to push our way on through school.

During the depression years of the 1930's when few young people could get jobs, most of them suffered these feelings of inferiority through no fault of their own. I had a student secretary then who worked half time and went to school the other half. She was a very ambitious girl who had developed the idea that money was the most important thing in the world.

Though she had been reared in a Southern home where the idea of "quality folk" was not based on money but on refinement and personal dignity, the experience of trying to climb in life without money had made her feel that money opened all doors.

Money is like a lot of things—it's terribly important if we don't have it, for it seems to be the tool for getting the things we want most. The desire for it is one of those things which time usually cures if we are ambitious, industrious, and thrifty, but while we are still on the way "up," poverty has its sting.

Tom's case is typical of that of many college students who are struggling to get along.

> Never having the things my friends had has always bothered me. They always had cars, summer trips, spending money, and other luxuries that I could not afford.
>
> They would do things for me such as giving me rides in their cars, taking me to movies, and inviting me to

dinners at their homes. Yet it has always seemed to me
that I've been under obligation to people. I have tried
in little ways to repay my friends but that doesn't seem
to help much.

Judy's case of inferiority was caused by her parents'
lack of understanding about the importance of clothes in
a girl's life. She writes:

> Clothes are very important to a girl. My parents could
> never understand how much they meant to me. While
> all my girl friends were buying, talking about, and plan-
> ning their wardrobes, I had only three different outfits
> to wear. To cover my feelings of inferiority from this I
> became very sarcastic, even in conversations not relating
> to clothes.
>
> Following my freshman year in college, I finally con-
> vinced them of my need, and after I had acquired the
> longed-for wearing apparel, I became more self-confident
> and my sarcasm and inferiority feelings soon vanished.

*Social deficiencies is the fourth field from which infe-
riority feelings arise.* There is an old saying which goes,
"It takes three generations to make a gentleman." The
great playwright George Bernard Shaw tried to prove this
in *Pygmalion* by having a college professor take it upon
himself to reeducate an ignorant flower girl in the niceties
of upper-class speech and manners, and then pass her off
as a member of this class. She got by for a while, but in the
end she fitted neither layer of society—the one of her birth
nor the one of her training.

We don't believe in gentlemen in the English sense and
have gone so far as to make titles of nobility illegal, yet

even in our very democratic society, as we move from one social setting to another, we often feel the pinch of our ignorance of manners and niceties. Perhaps we feel it more because we have no hard-and-fast social classes and move so freely into circles where we are not fully familiar with all the customs and manners. Sometimes we are not tough enough to take our blunders without feeling some intense pangs of inferiority. Few have escaped such feelings in our social system.

Avril's trouble began when his folks moved from the farm home, where he had always lived, to town. He writes:

> It was a different sort of life for me, with all my surroundings changed, my old friends gone, and so many new things and people to get used to.
>
> To make matters worse, I didn't fit in at all with the new fellows I met. I was soon fighting to defend myself from the remarks of the town boys who wore different clothes and a different haircut. My mother had always cut my hair and it didn't look too good to the boys who lived in town and went to the barber. The town girls would have nothing to do with me either, because I was such an odd looking "country hick." Being avoided by both boys and girls soon had its effect upon me. Their picking on me and making remarks soon made me feel that I was inferior to them. It has been a hard feeling to shake off.

Many young people from farms experience some severe adjustments when they first go from small to large schools where they encounter new groups with different standards. It may not be the clothes or the haircut, but there is often something about one that is different.

Hilda was an exchange student from Germany. Her feeling of social inadequacy was very strong, and kept her from enjoying many of the new experiences she had looked forward to. At the end of her sophomore year she looks back over the steps of her adjustment.

I felt awkward and out of place in the dormitory as well as the classroom during most of my freshman year. My clothing seemed completely inappropriate and I spent most of my allowance on American-made skirts and sweaters. My speech and manners, too, were unlike those of the other girls, and though I watched and imitated as best I could, still I made many embarrassing blunders. In class I hesitated to speak up and seldom expressed an opinion, even when called upon, for fear of sounding silly or making a mistake.

This fall, a Finnish girl moved into the dormitory. I've learned a great deal from her. She wears her foreign clothing with an air of pride. She participates in many activities and is always eager to voice her opinions. She, too, makes many blunders but she laughs with the others and tries again. She has endeared herself to all who know her because, while she is eager to learn about America and American customs, she is just as eager to remain loyal to her homeland and tell others of its many customs.

The most important thing I have learned from her is that to be "different" is not necessarily to be "inferior."

Sometimes being an only child makes it hard to feel at home in the various new groups we have to be a part of as our circle of acquaintances and our activities widen. Olive writes of this handicap in the development of her personality. She says, "I played alone a great deal when I was a child. When I got into school it was difficult for me to feel that I was an intimate part of any group."

As she grew older, her aloofness was giving her a reputation for snobbishness, yet she didn't want to be snobbish. It was only that she was afraid of being hurt by the group. Actually she was feeling great inferiority because of this handicap. Her aloofness was just a protective front.

"I often feel when in a group," she writes, "that people couldn't possibly want me around. Not feeling at ease among them, I can't put myself forward naturally. Of course, the group doesn't put itself out to relieve my embarrassment, as everyone is primarily interested in himself. This only intensifies my feeling of inferiority and makes me draw back into myself even further. It's all been a vicious circle."

She goes on to tell how she has been working at overcoming this complex by developing excellence in speech and manners, achieving a good scholastic standing, and being successful in other ways in order to increase her self-confidence.

When we come right down to an honest appraisal of ourselves, we all have some vague feelings of inferiority. They may not be complexes—nothing more in many cases than slight misgivings as to our adequacy in certain situations. What to do—that is the question.

We shall consider various possibilities in Chapter IV.

Getting Wise to Ourselves

What are our motives?

The great Aristotle. Greek philosopher and teacher, admonished his pupils, "Know thyself." He considered this the beginning of all wisdom.

Sometimes self-knowledge is a very painful thing. It may come to us quite by accident. Seldom do we seek it. Often it comes through others.

We are quite rational about everything we do, of course. So we may think. Actually, most of us are motivated in strange ways. The drives within us are deeply implanted in past experiences, frustrations, slights, and disappointments, as well as in happy experiences and satisfying successes. Human emotions have a way of trying to turn defeat into victory and of reacting to pain by trying out new adjustments that will help us avoid pain in the future.

This is as much true of emotional pain as of physical pain. When, as small children, we burn ourselves on something hot, we learn to keep our distance from heat. In the same way, if we get badly smitten with love and are unexpectedly let down, we don't permit our emotions to go so far again without knowing our ground. If we have

been badly defeated in any venture, we are less bold thereafter to rush in where angels fear to tread. Pain teaches us
caution.

Getting wise to ourselves will require some probing to
find the forces which give us drive. We may not find them
all, but we shall certainly recognize many of them, and
facing up to our real motives can be a most revealing experience. Some of us will find that the devotion and ad-
miration of others give us our will to succeed, but some
will find frustration and anxiety as the forces that push
them forward.

Don't be alarmed if all is not perfect

Drive in a human being is like a powerful dynamo,
throbbing with energy and force. Those with the most
drive have not been persons without frustrations or
problems.

Alfred Adler, whom we mentioned before as the inven-
tor of the concept inferiority complex, in addressing a
group of students at the University of Michigan some
years ago, advised us that all great achievement is explained by the inferiority complex. He cited many cases
from history to prove his point.

Although he presented a very convincing case, he was
probably wrong in attributing all greatness to inferiority
feelings. Yet the human personality is a peculiar thing.
If the body is well-fed and we have a sense of good health
and physical well-being, if we are completely at home in
the group and happy in all our relationships, it is easy to

become so satisfied that we drift along without drive or ambition.

From reading student autobiographies, one gets the impression that scholarship itself is often a compensation for some degree of failure in adjusting successfully to high school. Again and again one observes that the bright college student talks about having been poorly adjusted during his high-school years and having turned to books to help conquer his sense of failure in relationship with his age mates. Thus social inadequacies are frequently the driving force behind academic success. This, of course, is not always so.

The reasons for social rejection are different, but the consequences are usually quite similar. Most young people react as Terry did. She writes, "My parents felt it was out of the question for me to go to dances or run around with the gang. This just about broke my heart, but I was soon compensating by substituting high grades and leading my class in scholarship."

To give up or to fight

This much is to be said for Adler's view: The human personality has force within it to try to turn all defeats into victories, either by fighting failure directly or through some substitute activity that will bring a sense of personal satisfaction and vindicate us in our own eyes and in the eyes of the group.

Although all achievement is certainly not to be explained by inferiority feelings, inferiorities often do become the source of powerful drives that compel us to pour our energies into a strenuous compensative effort which will bring success. We are inclined to react to any kind of defeat or frustration by renewed striving in some direction.

With all of us, of course, there is a point at which the odds become too great. Neurotics are those who have been unable to convert their frustrations into constructive energy and to compensate successfully. They accept their defeat and tell themselves that it isn't worth the gamble, or sometimes they fix their frustrated thoughts and energies upon personally and socially worthless activities—fanatical cleanliness or perhaps completely unfounded fears and jealousies.

It is better to die fighting in the right direction than to be burned up by our own frustrations. Compensation, even if it does at times betray our desperate striving to survive as persons, is better than giving up in defeat and despair.

Take the experience of one boy after the divorce of his parents. His situation is not uncommon in today's world, yet he reacted by healthy, realistic compensation, rather than by sinking into defeat and self-pity. The divorce occurred during his first year of high school in a small rural community which had little tolerance for divorce and even condemned and avoided children who were in the families of divorced parents.

Ted writes of his compensation:

I needed something to make up for the loss of companionship of my father, and something to replace the satisfaction I was missing because I could not play with other children. The only way I could get this satisfaction was to excel my classmates and make them look up to me. So I began to study harder, work harder, and strive harder to fulfill this desire to excel. This is the reason that today I want to be the best athlete, the best student, and the most popular man; this is the reason I want to do greater things than anyone else; this goes back to the divorce of my parents with its attendant circumstances which developed in me a self-consciousness, preventing me from associating with other people, and leaving me, as the only outlet, a strong desire to excel other people.

Antisocial compensations

Of course, compensation may take less constructive forms. The young person who is shunned by classmates, who feels awkward or inferior, searches desperately for a new means of winning self-respect and the respect of others. The fortunate young person, the bright one or the one with adult help and guidance, will choose a form of compensation that brings him this respect. Others may not be so fortunate. Some find that the bully, the show-off, or the classroom nuisance can win the attention, if not the friendship, of others. As a result, the frustrated young person often turns to these antisocial forms of compensation, rather than to academic or athletic striving. This was the case with Claude, the runtiest boy in his class. He became so tough that the gang gave him first place.

"Nothing pleased me better," he writes, "than being elected leader of a Halloween party. I would do almost anything. We just reveled in getting the cops after us and annoying them. I was the boldest in the gang in this respect."

Correcting antisocial compensations

Aggressive reactions. Here is a child's aggressive reactions to being thrown into a larger group than the one to which she was accustomed. Not knowing how to adjust, she fights out her frustrations, striking against those about her.

> When I had graduated from the sixth grade, I attended Clover Park Intermediate, which was a larger school, having almost two hundred pupils. This time the process of adjustment was harder, for the students came from farther places. Again the conflict arose in that I wanted attention and wasn't getting it. To obtain attention I gleefully tripped all unfortunate students who walked too close to me. After a while the pupils began to be cautious whenever they saw me coming. As I became better acquainted and began to like my teachers, I lost interest in that sort of thing.

As one reads the above account, he wonders if this girl would have given up her antisocial behavior had some unwise teacher caught her tripping other children and punished her. The wise teacher would, of course, have interpreted this behavior as a symptom of personality difficulties, rather than an indication of meanness.

Mary Jane writes of feeling inferior to her younger sister and describes the antisocial compensations she developed.

> I wonder if Jeannie will ever really forgive me and feel close to me as most sisters do. Ours is the old story of

conflict between the older girl and her younger, prettier sister. I was the older girl in this case and Jeannie was smarter, lovelier, kinder, and much more popular than I, ever since I can remember.

The real problem started, I believe, when I was about nine, and my mother turned over Jeannie's care to me. I had to help her dress, keep her clean, and take her with me wherever I went. Everyone fell under Jeannie's charm almost at sight, and I played second fiddle both at home and among our neighborhood playmates.

I can remember trying to hurt her in every way I could and then feeling terrible because she never blamed me or, if she did, never told on me. I'd tie her shoes too tightly so they would hurt her, or I'd yank the comb through her hair until tears came to her eyes. Once when I was teaching her to swim I even held her under water until both of us became so frightened we started crying.

I got along well in high school until my junior year, when she became a freshman. Right away she was the darling little Greer girl who could do everything better than anyone else, and still keep them as friends. I couldn't torture her physically any more, of course, but I did everything I could to tear down her reputation and win away her friends. I lost most of my friends in the process and got a reputation for being insincere, jealous, and a show-off.

Here at college I'm away from Jeannie for the first time since she was born. I'm beginning to understand why I felt toward her and acted as I did. How often I wish that my mother or one of my high-school teachers had had enough insight to understand what was wrong and help me out.

· I know now that if Jeannie and I are ever together again, I'll be able to hold my own in winning and keeping friends. Being away from her I've developed in talents and looks, poise, and, most of all, self-confidence.

Tolerance for others. We are sometimes intolerant of friends and new acquaintances because they overact so much in an attempt to get attention. We may misunderstand their motives and think they are supreme egotists. Often they are merely compensating to fight off feelings of inferiority.

If we can give them genuine friendliness, often the obnoxious traits disappear. Friendliness is what they really want but don't quite know how to go about getting it.

Extreme pride, snobbishness, bullying, loudness, showing off, or overdressing and too much make-up are some of the many ways in which young people, and adults too, try to cover up feelings of inferiority. They are ways of displaying a bold, self-confident front when we actually feel weak and uncertain about ourself and our standing.

These are ways in which one who has been hurt has of covering up. Let us look at some cases which illustrate this point. The first is of a boy who, as an only child, never learned to live with playmates. He wanted their friendship but had not learned how to get along in the give-and-take world of adolescence. His compensations took him away from what he really wanted, as he saw later when writing his autobiography.

Because I was the only child and my dad was making a fairly good living, I was able to afford a better bicycle and spend a little more money on candy and things than my playmates. This separated me from them, and being in a small community, I could not find new friends to replace those I so rapidly lost. I became independent and kept to myself, read books for recreation, and attempted to make playmates jealous by the new bicycle, clothes, and extra money. That this was the wrong way to get what I wanted, and did not work, can easily be seen. The teachers at school, if they recognized the problem, did nothing; and there was no group leader to help. I think that if teachers and children's leaders were trained to look for and correct social maladjustments, like mine and others, they would be doing a great service to many individuals.

The following case is of a young woman who had been used to compensating for her uncertain position in the group by loudness, which often led to the embarrassment and humiliation of others. She describes the moment when she got wise to herself and in a very real sense became converted to a new moral nature. Joanne tells it this way:

Because of my undersized leg, I acted silly most of the time, being not literally "loud," but nevertheless, I know now I would have heartily disliked anyone who acted as I did. I was the typical "funny man" of our class and was often even brutal and mean toward others. At about fourteen years of age I obtained an ugly view of myself which cured me instantly. I was walking with Bernadette, an older friend of mine, when we met June, a shy, gangling girl of about thirteen. I piped up with, "Hello, Bones!"

I thought it was very funny. Bernadette, however,

looked at me shocked, and said, "Do you know, that would have hurt me terribly."

I tried to cover it over but the damage had been done and I knew it well. Nothing was said about the matter after that, but it was the last nasty remark I ever intentionally made to anyone.

Here is another girl who looks back on her high-school days with some embarrassment at the attention-getting role she played:

At first the big school was fun, but soon the novelty wore off and I felt ill at ease among so many. It was at this time that I went about achieving status in another way. I pounced upon "personality" books and indulged in daydreams of me as a sparkling individual, just too, too popular. I read some "slush" which said men didn't like their women to be too intelligent. Armed with such notions, I started acting the role of a silly, frivolous girl. I always managed to be in the center of a group of boys; and other girls, not knowing how asinine I was behaving, envied me. But I know now that the boys thought I was terribly affected with all my silly prattle. After the noon hour was over, I would go to my classes feeling unhappily discontented. The situation took care of itself when one boy of whom I was particularly fond began to be interested in me. When I was going out regularly with him, I regained my lost self-confidence and adopted a more natural attitude.

We often feel ashamed of our past when we become aware that we have used adjustment devices that put us in a bad light. But this is life, and there will never be a time when we will not in one place or another try to play into the limelight in ways that we will later regret.

We do more of this in youth than later, for being uncertain of our status then, we have to try out many devices in winning a place for ourselves. But we have all seen adults do the same thing when they wanted very badly to make an impression.

The author remembers watching a woman force her way through a crowd to grasp Mrs. Eleanor Roosevelt by the hand, as this First Lady was being hurriedly ushered out of a lecture hall. It seemed most rude. Mrs. Roosevelt greeted the woman kindly and hurried on to her next engagement.

Perhaps the woman, whoever she was, so worshipped this great lady that she couldn't resist the urge to grasp her hand. More than likely she wanted to boast to her bridge or sewing club that she had shaken hands with the President's wife.

Live and learn

There is an old saying to the effect that "Rome was not built in a day." The same might be said of personality.

As youth, we need not feel ashamed of some blundering in trying to find or win our place in the social group. Learning to fit the group and developing the personality traits which help us to fit it are somewhat like learning to play a complicated game like baseball or basketball. One can hardly expect to learn without making many errors in the process and committing a good many blunders.

A balance of success and failure

We are fortunate indeed if life hands us a balanced portion of success and failure. Psychologists and educators discuss among themselves what the proper balance is. One ventures fifty-fifty; another says two-thirds success and one-third failure; still another, four-fifths success and one-fifth failure.

The facts are that no one knows just how much failure is required to keep us striving to be our best. Sometimes a very small percentage of failure in an all-important area almost overwhelms us.

In our early college years we have one great factor in our favor: *Time.* We are still growing, and many failures can be mended as we grow on toward the years of fuller responsibility.

CHAPTER V

Flying Away to Dreamland

The psychology of escape

My name is Carol. Although I am in college, I still feel like a little girl on tiptoe looking into a warm room of companionship through a cold window of loneliness. If people knew I felt that way, they would say it was impossible for a child in a family of seven to feel alone, but I can assure them that it is only too real. I was born on a farm near Kansas City, Missouri, in a very close-knit family group. Every Sunday I was queen of a large gathering of relatives, since I was the only small child in the group, but this high status was soon shattered as the family increased in size. When we moved from Kansas to a Western state, my real loneliness began. There we had no relatives and there were no friends. My father had a low-paying job. The family steadily increased in size. With each new arrival there was a tightening of the family budget and new responsibility was placed on me.

For as long as I can remember, I have been given the responsibility of all my younger brothers and sisters. I have never been a child playing with them. I have always been a small and efficient overseer. My brothers and sisters soon regarded me as someone to hide from because

49

35562

they couldn't have fun when I was around. When the family went to town on Saturday, I was hardly ever allowed to go along. My parents didn't want to be bothered with all of the children so left some behind for Carol to take care of. They always assumed that Carol could not only take care of herself but also of the younger ones. "Leave Carol" is a phrase I learned to hate. I became indifferent to my parents and was unable to play with children my own age. I simply did not know how to get along with them. More and more I withdrew within myself. For the lack of affection of my parents and lack of association with others, I compensated in daydreams and by stroking the more sensitive parts of my body. As I grew older, I retired further and further within myself and played fascinating games in my imagination.

Carol's world was too severe for her. She created another. We can be quite sure that it was, in most repects, the opposite of the one in which she had been forced to live.

What our daydreams mean

We all dream, but unless life has mistreated us rather badly, we probably have not felt the need to escape so far from reality as Carol did.

The boy with lots of interesting dates doesn't spend much time dreaming about the princess who comes out of nowhere to meet all his emotional needs. It is the one who cannot date succesfully who dreams about the perfect date.

In this sense at least, our daydreams help us understand ourselves. They center around things we wish to realize in real life, or they carry us away from our failures to a cre-

ated world in which we always play a distinctive and satisfying role. This is why daydreaming is often referred to as
"wishful thinking."

Daydreams can carry us farther and farther away from
reality and into the imaginative, or they can be constructive, leading to plans for action and avenues for escape
from our frustrations.

The daydreams of college freshmen, particularly during
the first month or so of the semester, are filled with impossibly lovely pictures of home and the old home town.
Mothers are likely to be remembered as the greatest cooks
and fathers as the most generous and understanding dads
a person could ever ask for. Everything about home takes
on a special glow of perfection, and forgotten are the argu-
ments and frustrations that made us so impatient to be out
on our own.

This kind of daydreaming, of course, is a result of homesickness. Our memory contrasts our present lost feeling
and our difficulties with the pleasant recollections of our
childhood home. When we come right down to it, home
was never quite the perfect place we feel it was at such
moments. But the illusion persists in our imagination.

A college counselor of my acquaintance urged the sororities on her campus to do away with the rule forbidding
freshmen to return home for visits.

"Don't think for a minute that your restrictions are
helping freshmen to overcome their homesickness," she
argued. "Home becomes twice as wonderful when it is put
off-limits." She went on to suggest, "When you see a sad-
eyed, listless freshman, tell her to go home and stay for as

long as she can. In a few days she will be so bored with the old town, so eager to get back into the swing of things, that she will hurry back, her homesickness cured."

Reasons for daydreaming

The chronic daydreamer usually has some rather serious reasons for this habit. Miss Day, whose analysis of hundreds of student autobiographies was previously referred to, concluded that there are at least five reasons for it. She found that it usually resulted from (1) lack of success in obtaining affection from parents or friends, (2) being excluded from a desired group, (3) lack of success in making grades, in athletics, or in some form of competition, (4) lack of finances or of acceptable clothes or some other humiliating shortages, (5) lack of success in dating.

Of these five things, lack of affection and acceptance seems to be the most important one in driving a person to fantasy.

Daydreaming may take creative forms—art, music, reading—when these are used as ways of escape.

"I was a shy, bashful fellow," Seth writes, "and I did not feel at all equal to the bolder and more polished men I met here at college. I felt awkward and out of place from the beginning, and always imagined people were staring at my clothes and talking about my manners. In order to keep my spirits up I told myself again and again that the others were just show-offs who didn't really deserve my friendship anyway. As a result, I began to withdraw further and further into the realm of imagination, and I became a devotee of the public library, frequently reading an entire book in an evening. I imagined myself in the role of the hero, the envied artist, the brilliant conversationalist, and many and strange were the things which I fancied myself doing.

"As a matter of fact, this withdrawal was not all for the worst. Reading gave me a new and better vocabulary, new interests and insights, and something to talk about. Within a few months I began to discover that I could hold my own in most conversations and felt at ease among the brighter students, even though I still felt out of place with the social lions."

The results of withdrawals to the world of books and make-believe are not always so favorable. Many young people find this world so satisfying that they remain content to dream rather than to do. The beauty of this world is that if the parts do not suit, one can lay the book aside and choose another with parts which do. Real life is not always so accommodating.

Unlike Seth, Gladys typifies the many who use the world of fancy to avoid making the real adjustments demanded by life in our present-day world.

"There has always been one means of escape for me," Gladys writes. "If my attitudes and beliefs don't fit in with those of other people, if I feel very much abused, if the status accorded me is not what I want, then I don't have to stay and take it. At any time I can pick up a book or a magazine and very shortly be in another world, or at least in someone else's world than my own. I know that when those people found happiness it was complete and not plagued by doubts as is mine. If I can identify myself with them for a while, then I can face my own world with a more balanced outlook."

Mabel reflects her isolated upbringing in a rural community by her daydreaming of a world peopled as she chooses.

A small creek ran by the apple orchard just back of the house. This was the "Garden of Eden" for me. Many of the happiest hours of my life were spent in the rather wild underbrush of the woods on the creek banks, playing with my dolls at times, but mostly alone, allowing my imagination to run riot in dreams and pretended happenings. I never expressed them aloud to other people. Today, I daydream to quite an extent, constructing all sorts of wonderful impossible activities. All my life I have compensated for my very ordinary existence by daydreams. Emotional attitudes, with the exception of the love of my family, have been comparatively absent or consciously not permitted to develop. As a compensation, I have developed elaborate imaginary situations emphasizing my superiority. These dreams are very quickly dispelled, however, by any activity, physical action, or association with other people.

Lou is driven to her dream world by real or imagined slights of her peers.

In grade school and even in high school the "snubs" of my schoolmates would be pondered over and over in my mind for a long time, although they would soon be forgotten by the others. I found it very hard to accept the fact that certain people would be very cool one day and very chummy the next with no apparent reason. I drew more and more into my shell and turned to fantasy thinking for consolation. My parents kept telling me to "get down to earth," and many people thought I was snobbish. That was not the case at all. I just lived in two worlds and found the imaginary one much more interesting. I avoided social functions, although in my dream world I attended many, and at each I was the "belle of the ball." I wanted to go out and have good times like others my own age, but instead I sublimated my desires and became very interested in reading modern fiction.

Girls and boys differ

Girls more often than boys mention daydreaming in their autobiographies. Girls apparently use it as an adjustment device more than boys. Perhaps this is because boys more often take a job to fill their spare time, or are more often required to work around home. Perhaps, too, girls are a little more romantic and think more of love and of relationships with others. Boys are more likely to be engaged in work with things and to have less concern about their relationships with people.

Another circumstance may also contribute to this difference. Girls feel greater pressure to attain social success than do boys. They are expected to cultivate poise, manners, and good looks. They are likely to feel that they are inferior if they do not date or have many close friends. Boys are more often forgiven their awkwardness, their shyness, or their looks. If they do not date, it is considered their own business and seldom a sign of inferiority. As a result, they are less likely to turn to daydreams because of social failures and frustrations.

Among those who do engage in fantasy, the dreams of boys are found to be somewhat different from those of girls. Boys' daydreams are much more likely to deal with the work they would like to do or with other activities that will bring them greatness, success, or fame.

"I often lie in bed," Ted writes, "and sort of dream of what I would like to be. One night I will imagine myself as a great athlete, and then a big businessman, and other times a great explorer. I do believe there isn't any harm in this, and it does take my mind off other problems."

Are daydreams good or bad?

Daydreams are neither good nor bad. It all depends on how much they are used and what they are used for.

As a cushion for our failures and a solace for emotional pain, they have a place in all our personalities. They become undesirable when we substitute them for the real world to such an extent that we fail to make the adjustments which should be made.

As we grow older, we should dream less and act more. As we choose our part in life, as we establish definite goals ahead, we shall more often know what we must do to reach them. This makes choices easier and helps us replace dreams with positive action.

If we persist in dreaming, we should analyze ourselves and, if necessary, seek counseling help to learn whether the wishes being thwarted can be realized or whether, with maturity, we should abandon them as a part of childhood.

Daydreams and your college life

Daydreams are probably no more common among college students than among other young people of the same age, but a special note of warning should be added here concerning the dangers of daydreams to your college life.

First of all, dreaming takes time, especially daydreams. Psychologists tell us that our dreams at night, while they seem to last for hours, often take but a few seconds. Just the opposite is true of daydreams; we may spend hours dreaming about our one big moment. College life is fast-moving. There are books which must be read, papers which must be written, as well as activities that demand much of our time and energy. Most college students scarcely find time in a sixteen-hour day to finish all their studies and activities. As a result, the daydreamer is almost certain to miss out on something important while he is away in dreamland.

Second, and of greater importance, are the psychological consequences of too much daydreaming. When we do not reach our goal, when we feel discouraged, frustrated, or that we have failed, we have two choices: (1) We may sit and dream about how grand it would have been had we succeeded, or (2) we may reconsider our plans and objectives, remap our course, and try again.

Even the best students and the most popular young people are likely to feel failure and frustration during their college days. Not all term papers deserve an A, and even the popular student cannot win every office and honor he may desire. As a result, daydreaming is a temptation constantly lurking near at hand. To give up, to turn away from the cold, ugly facts and bask in the warmth of "used to be" or "might have been," is an easy step to take. But the rewards are greater and far more lasting in the world of reality.

Knowing that this temptation very probably lies ahead may help many a college freshman prepare to meet his disappointments with renewed energies and a determination not to let his dreams carry him out of this world.

CHAPTER VI

A New Looking Glass

We see our image reflected in new groups

Every new group of people represents a new looking glass in which we see our image reflected back to us. Most of us grew up in neighborhoods where we were well known and had a definite place in the lives of our family and friends. The image of ourselves reflected in the old group was clear, familiar, and probably flattering. But now we are in college, surrounded by strangers who know very little about us and seem to care even less. The image we see reflected is cold and impersonal; it probably shows more of our faults and defects than we care to admit having.

"For the first time in my life," Lucile writes of her college experience, "I have been away from the influence of my parents and my brother, Louis. I have found that I have to sink or swim, and it is up to me which it will be. My parents have always showed their appreciation for any work I did, but since I have been 'on my own' I have learned that I must do things even if they do not seem to be appreciated.

"The change from home to college life is the biggest

change I have ever experienced," she concludes. "My picture of myself has gone down to a smaller scale, and the field of cooperation and competition is much larger and harder. Becoming adjusted to people and getting settled among these new people and groups is my biggest problem."

The awakening was even worse for Jerry who left a farm for a large city university. He tells how he felt when he "plunged into city living with practically no idea of what cities were even like."

"The city," he continues, "was so entirely different from the country. Things moved more rapidly and urban ways were new and different. The standards of behavior in the city differed considerably from those of my home town. I found it hard to adjust myself. I soon found that urban people had broader ideas and more of them. They seemed so sure of themselves. The thing I needed most to help me in this situation was what I had least of: self-confidence."

This is the cold, cold world

In an earlier day when parents were sending their children out to face life alone, they described the world out beyond the home town as a cold world. It need not be, but it does expect us to measure up. It doesn't excuse us for our failures or let us get by as did the more sympathetic group in our childhood surroundings. As a youngster, among our home-town friends many of our mistakes or failures were excused. "You tried," they comforted us; or "Well, you're still young; you'll know better next time." Here at college we shall be judged largely by our accomplishments, not by our efforts or good intentions. The hurdles are a little higher, but the joys of true accomplishment are greater, too.

"At the beginning of my college career, I was sadly disillusioned," Corrine writes. "I soon learned that things weren't going to be as they had been at home. They wouldn't give in to me when I wanted my own way. People aren't so eager to please. Everything has always come so easily before, it doesn't seem that the world is treating me just right these days."

Bruce writes, "I came up here with the idea that I was rather a big shot, but was soon awakened to the fact that I am simply one of several thousand college students. They haven't noticed what a great guy I am yet. I'm beginning to doubt that I'm such a big shot after all."

Carl concludes, "I find the college group hard to break into and many times get disgusted. I feel like giving up, but I imagine what folks at home would say of me if I quit, so I stay with it. I haven't time for boxing, my favorite sport. Being a pledge in a fraternity has tended to give me an inferiority complex. I feel I am looked down on by the upperclassmen and not treated as their equal. But I have made a vow to see it through."

The adult image in the looking glass

Early in college we begin to have to make decisions for ourselves. No adult is at hand to guide us, and we suddenly become aware that we are expected to act like mature persons. While we may not recognize it as such, this is one of the first symptoms of adulthood.

Maturity consists primarily in our being willing and able to face life as adults in three spheres of behavior: (1) the moral, (2) the economic, and (3) our relationships with the opposite sex.

We must now make moral choices. As children, others defined good and bad for us. We accepted their definitions and acted as our parents wished, or contrary to their wishes and suffered the consequences. They were our conscience and our policemen. If we made others suffer for our wrongdoing, our parents had to face the consequences. Now, with the approach of maturity, we are for the first time being expected to make moral choices. Our own conscience must be our guide, and we must suffer a secret remorse for violating it. And if we commit external acts that violate the rules, society expects us to face our punishment as a man or woman. It excuses children, not adults.

Many are still dependent in an economic sense, even though in most societies—and in an earlier day, in our own society—they would have been expected to have made their own way. Now final economic maturity usually comes at marriage rather than at fourteen, sixteen, or eighteen years of age. Yet college is the time when all young people who have not already done so begin to take steps that lead to economic maturity. Many have already worked, earned, and saved. Some are already paying their way in full. For them, economic maturity has come. For others, it has come only partially, and for some not at all.

Economic maturity is not just a matter of earning, saving, and spending wisely. It consists in certain attitudes toward work and productive usefulness. No one wants to be idle and to fail to contribute his share to society through work. Those whose parents can and are putting them through college should, as a step toward maturity, develop mature attitudes concerning the use of both money and time.

Children are expected to play and trifle away time in useless activity. Adults who do so are parasites. Mature attitudes require that we begin to put work, duty, and responsibility to the foremost. Play and social activity begin to take a secondary place and to fit into their own restricted time. Work becomes the major activity of life for us as it is and must always be for adults. We shall have more to say about this later.

Finally, there is that matter of adult relationships with the opposite sex. This transition is one in which affections and interests gradually are transferred from our immediate family to members of the opposite sex and finally to one member of the opposite sex, who will in time with us create a new family. The transition to marital maturity should begin with more serious dating and the eventual development of adult attitudes toward marriage with an understanding of the role and responsibilities of husband and wife.

We shall have much more to say about this important transition also in later chapters.

Deciding things for yourself is the beginning
 of adulthood

College students in their own way sense the beginnings
of adult responsibility early in their college experience.
It comes to one in one way and to another in another way,
but this awakening to new responsibilities is apparent in
their autobiographical accounts.

"I missed the important feeling of a high-school senior
and felt instead the unimportant feeling of a college freshman," Esther writes of her first days in college. "All decisions, whether major or minor, had to be made by myself
alone. Neither my father nor mother were here to seek advice from. The meaning of independence was becoming
clear to me. When I did turn home seeking advice, which
to me seemed very important, my folks wisely managed to
leave the final decision up to me."

"When I finally arrived at college I was rather bewildered," Marcia admits. "So many decisions had to be made
by me alone; neither my father nor mother could suggest
a solution for every little situation. So many things were
involved. For instance, should I schedule my difficult
courses for the first semester or so and get them over with,
or should I put them off until another year and concentrate on good grades and getting acquainted?"

The many adjustments of being on one's own in college
are suggested by Yvonne.

> As was expected, my first reaction to college life was
> negative—never before had I encountered so many people
> with such divergent ideas. Although I had begun to go

ahead somewhat, still this was completely "paddle my own canoe." I had to make my decision on the right things to buy and to conserve as much as possible. I missed the quiet life which I had led and which had offered few of the many decisions that now faced me. A roommate was quite a different person from a sister—with her you must share the room as well as maintain good study habits and good conversational relationships.

Evelyn still hasn't reached the point where she can make decisions with confidence. "During most of my life," she writes, "my parents have made my important decisions for me, and now that I must decide some things for myself, I find it very difficult. I haven't chosen a major because I don't know which one to choose. My abilities and skills seem to be just about equally divided among all the fields. What I will do in the future is a major question for me."

Then she expresses her fear: "Unless I can decide which way to go soon, I will probably turn out to be another no-body—just what I have always been afraid of."

Patty, although starting out with the same handicap—that of having parents who decided everything for her—has made the shift to independence of adulthood. She writes:

The most important thing that happened to me was starting college. I wasn't a bit thrilled about coming to college. It has taken me quite a while to adjust myself to the rules. Down here I am completely on my own. Before, my parents helped me to make decisions on various problems. Now that I am at college I have become less dependent on them and I have cleared up some of my mental conflicts. Down here at school I have learned to act and think for myself.

Give yourself time and talk things over

Don't be too discouraged and impatient at your awkwardness in taking over the reins of your own life. Some students can do it easily because they have had greater independence at home or because they are older or temperamentally more suited for complete self-direction. But for most of us, the problems of independence are almost as great as its joys. The roommate may put on a smooth, self-assured front, but likely as not, he (or she) is just as worried as you, constantly wondering, "Now, what would Mom tell me to do if she were here."

Fortunately for us, the problem is an old one. Nowadays colleges and universities know that most of their freshman class will be worried over how to use their new independence and how to make decisions in the absence of Mom and Dad. Most institutions provide special counselors for freshmen, not only to help with academic problems but also with personal and social ones. We may talk things over with these counselors with the full assurance of their sincere interest and complete confidence.

CHAPTER VII

Sweet Liberty

Freedom has its price

An ancient philosopher once said that our troubles begin when we are free to do as we please. It has always been so.

Christ told of the prodigal son who decided to take his share of the inheritance and leave home to do as he pleased. He had his big time, spent the inheritance, and ended up so desperate that he was taking his meals in the pig lot, stealing food from the swine. Finally he came back home and admitted that his father's ways were best after all. It took all this to make him see life as a mature adult must if he is to fit into the society of human beings.

It is often very difficult for us to learn that conventions are for our protection, not just to harness us and keep us from doing what we please. Some years ago the author studied the history of three mining towns. In the early days life was cheap there, where men did much as they pleased. Many men who would have practiced sobriety in a more restrained environment literally drank themselves to death. They had not learned to live wisely with liberty.

They could not exercise self-imposed restraints where outside control was weak.

Social revolt is normal for youth

Revolt is a normal reaction of young people to the restraints of childhood and the early teens. The extent to which we need to rebel, to set ourselves free from these old restraints, depends on the extent to which our actions have been unreasonably curbed. A few generations ago when family discipline was much more rigid than now, parents more or less expected that their young people would sow "wild oats" when they got away from the strong parental rule. Few moved away from home in those days, so wild oats was not a major crop.

Nowadays most of us grow up in families that are quite democratic. We have always had considerable freedom of choice and do not feel the need of serious rebellion when we get away and are on our own for the first time. Yet I know from reading many autobiographies of students that a great many of them do experience at least a mild period of rebellion.

They may act much as do some young men in the armed forces. It being their first venture from home, they cut loose there and do a lot of things they later regret. Usually a little time and maturity cure them.

In college, the spree of doing what one pleases often takes the form of having a good time at the expense of studies. The student ends up the first semester on probation. After a talk with the reinstatement committee he may achieve some maturity. If he does not, likely as not the middle of the second semester sees him on his way back home, "flunked out" of college.

This book is not a sermon. Emancipation from home is a necessary step toward growing up in our kind of world, where in adulthood we shall be largely on our own, living and supporting ourselves away from parents. The zest for freedom must be found before one can make any claims to adulthood. But, of course, freedom places upon us the necessity of making choices, with all the responsibilities they entail.

"When I got to college," Henry writes, "I took advantage of the opportunity to 'improve' my personality and sowed a few wild oats in doing so." He tells how he went about seeking these "improvements":

> Whereas I had formerly been rather reserved and shy, I now became the loud-mouthed extrovert; where before I had been moderate in my habits, I now became a nervous chain smoker and boisterous drinker. I also made up my mind that I was going to go to dances and go out with girls until I overcame my shyness. This was not too difficult to do as most men were still in the service, and there were four times as many girls as there were fellows. As a result of the aforementioned "improvements" in my personality, a few weeks after the beginning of the semester I was going with three girls, averaging two dances a week end, and drinking a little too heartily for my own good.

Hank's autobiographical sketch not only shows his rebellion against parental standards but also his gradual realization of a new set of standards after the rebellion died down. He writes:

I grew up on a not-too-prosperous farm in a family and neighborhood in which hard work and serious thoughts were considered to be the only virtues worth cultivating. Here at college the social life puts a premium upon the ability to make light, trivial conversation and to do as little work as possible. Needless to say, my adjustment was not an easy one.

At first, I was awed by the strange, new atmosphere. I couldn't understand how people in an institution of higher learning could act so giddy and carefree. Still I wanted very much to "fit in," so I covered up my overly serious disposition and tried to appear casual about my schoolwork.

Being new at the game of deception, I naturally over-played my part. Instead of moderately altering my stand-ards and behavior, I tossed all my past training to the winds. The hard-earned money with which I had planned to start a collection of worth-while books was soon spent on beer, cigarettes, and extravagant corsages to impress the girls.

My moment of awakening came the night after we re-ceived our first-semester grade cards. I had just returned to the dorm after attending a "beer bust" at which I had been presented a make-shift trophy (an elaborately trimmed beer bottle). Upon the trophy was written: "To Hank whose two D's and two F's testify to a semester well spent."

I laughed heartily with the rest of them but later that night, in the quiet of the dorm, I could ignore my con-science no longer. The ridiculous extreme to which I had stooped in order to "fit in" filled me with shame.

After hours of self-analyzing, during which I considered

many possible courses of action (including stepping completely out of all the college's social life), I finally decided to work out a schedule which would allow ample time for class preparation and some time for outside activities. Of course, I was particularly concerned about how my straight-laced parents would react to the grade slip. I decided that the only thing to do was to explain what had actually happened and why I had acted as I did.

The reply I received from my father a few days later is now one of my most cherished possessions. Here are a few lines from his letter:

". . . and if you have really profited by this experience, if you are ready to plan your days, allowing time and energy for the frills as well as the fabric of life, then your first semester may not have been completely wasted after all. In fact, it may have been one of the most important and profitable periods of your life. We are not all so fortunate in learning the lesson you have acquired while we are still young enough to profit by it."

Colleges have regulations, too

Many adolescents passing through the stage of revolt against parental authority eagerly await college as an escape from the many rules and regulations of home and the home town. These young people are generally in for a big surprise. Colleges, too, have their rules, and college personnel are seldom as lax and lenient as parents when it comes to enforcing them. There are regulations governing behavior, activities, and hours. There are places you must go and others that are forbidden. There are hours for rising and retiring, for eating and studying, for dating and for recreation. Most of us find that college actually confronts us with more rules and regulations than our moms and dads ever thought of.

The new freedom we enjoy is freedom to think for ourselves, to plan for ourselves and our futures, to face problems and make decisions away from direct parental interference. But this does not mean we are completely on our own. In place of Mom and Dad there are a dozen or so teachers, counselors, housemothers, and school administrators, who are vitally concerned about us and our lives. Still, within the limitations set by the institution, most of us will feel freer than we have ever felt before.

Getting along with liberty

So now you are free at last (or at least you feel that way). This new liberty is very much like a new machine or gadget—we want to see just what we can do with it. We have observed through the experiences of other college students that testing out this new freedom frequently brings clashes with our families or at least with the standards and codes given us by our families. There are other likely pitfalls, as June's autobiography suggests.

> I have felt and behaved very much like a spring which has been wound tight and then suddenly released. All my life I've been encouraged to read widely but my opinions have never been invited or, I should say, permitted, in family discussions. Here, at last, in college I found an audience. Professors seemed to encourage free discussion on controversial topics, and I responded to their encouragement like a hungry child at dinner. I argued with

anyone who had an opinion, and seldom hesitated to monopolize as much class time as I needed to expound my ideas. The professors were very courteous, so I assumed I had the green light to go ahead.

One day when the bell rang at the end of my Economics I class, I gathered my books up as usual and started to leave. The fellow who sat behind me touched my arm and said, "I think you've forgotten something."

I looked around my seat but it was clear, so I looked up questioningly.

He said, "Your soap box."

I don't know what he expected but certainly not the pain and humiliation I felt and must have shown. He was immediately embarrassed and apologetic, but the damage, or more accurately, the good, was already done.

The next class meeting I was quiet as a mouse and was amazed to see how many other students had something to say when I was not talking.

June discovered, as all of us will, that liberty is something most college students have only recently acquired and that she was not the only one eager to air her ideas and opinions before a courteous, respectful audience.

Loves and liberty

Liberty, to the young person, is a word with more than a whisper of romance in it. It brings thoughts of new adventures filled with wonderful new people (all of them handsome or beautiful, needless to say). So college is usually greeted as an adventure in romance as well as in the world of books and knowledge. Mom and Dad, of course, are no longer around to put the stamp of approval and disap-

proval on our friendships, so things really do look bright
and interesting.

It is true that we are likely to meet some very special
people in college, and perhaps even *the* very special person. But it is not true that colleges are overrun with a
unique breed of supermen and supergirls. The standards
that were important in choosing or accepting a date during
high school are equally or more important in college. Not
only your choice of dates but also your behavior on dates
are more than ever up to you. Mom won't hear about the
way you acted, and an indiscriminately given kiss is not
likely to be the gossip of the town. There are fewer specific
controls over just what you must and must not do on a date.
This merely means that you must take over more of the
responsibilities yourself. You demand of yourself and your
dates the standards of behavior you have been taught to
respect.

If these standards are ignored, both your reputation and
your self-respect are in for deflation.

Be informed about sex

One of the great deficiencies of our culture has been the
lack of any standard and certain procedure for teaching the
young the facts of life honestly and naturally, as we do
other aspects of physiology. Many even enter college ignorant of sex, with perverted and dirty ideas about it, or
with a feeling of shame connected with it, all because they
were not taught frankly and honestly so that they can accept sex as normal, natural, and wholesome when given its
proper place.

Here is an account of a young man's struggles with sex. He had been taught that the stork brings babies and given other sex knowledge on this level.

Sex was a subject of great interest on the school ground, especially among the older boys. I began to pick up such terms as "sexual intercourse," "pregnancy," "passion," "slut," to say nothing of a great many "more vulgar" terms. I began to acquire a knowledge of sex, most of which was very fallacious.

As soon as I reached the age of puberty I began to feel the sex drive. I was ashamed of this feeling because I thought it was wrong to even experience it. It kept growing stronger and stronger. Thoughts of sex began to creep into my mind. Girls began to mean someone with whom to have sexual relations. Before long, any story containing sex, or a moving picture, or even just to look at a girl, would arouse all these urges and drives until I was undergoing the most serious conflict of my life.

To find relief I began to indulge in masturbation. This wasn't enough! I started to daydream—to imagine that I was fulfilling my sex urges naturally, and what it would feel like. My mind became filled with filth, fallacious ideas, sex relationships, passion. I could not help myself. I tried to shut these guilty thoughts out of my mind, but they crept in, slyly, insidiously, and I could not get them out. Every story I would read had sex in it, every show I would see had sex in it, and every girl I would look at meant sex. I even tried to shut these thoughts out of mind, but they would come out in my dreams. All I could think of was sex.

By indulging in daydreams I escaped the conflict between my sex urge and the actual codes so that I didn't actually fulfill these urges in sexual relations. But my mind was still filled with these thoughts. I had been taught from childhood that it was wrong to even think of sex, to talk about it, or to even feel any sex urges. I thought it was a sin in the eyes of God, and I must not let anyone know about it. I had to do something to relieve this conflict, or go *crazy*. I soon began to rationalize, giving myself good reasons why this urge should jibe with religion. I would say that religion is old-fashioned about sex; that if God made man, He also gave man his organic drives; and if God gave man his organic drives, why should God's religion make it a sin for these drives to be experienced? The conflict was so extreme that the only way I could have any peace of mind at all was to separate the two entirely. That is what I did. Slowly, through these rationalizations, I fenced the two off, completely divorcing sex from my religious beliefs. I still believe in God and in His teachings. I still experience sex drives. But the two no longer conflict, because they are entirely separated one from the other.

A girl writes of the way her mother informed her about sex and the damage done in hindering her normal associations with men:

The facts of life were presented to me in a small book called the *Light of the World*—or something equally disgusting to my child mind. I mentally revolted against the way the truth was set down and suffered no little mental agony. To this day I get a sick feeling when I think of that book. I sometimes want to blame my mother for this, but Mother had never had sex explained to her and knew no other way of presenting it. When I look back now it doesn't seem possible that it could affect me so, but something about it made me shy of men. I have since overcome this idea concerning sex and can talk freely about it, but the first impressions still persist and keep me from complete freedom with men unless I know them very well.

The following is the account of a girl who had had such rigid taboos built into her personality that she should have revolted against much of her teaching in order to be free, but she was too well bound by it ever to revolt successfully. She tells her story:

In the convent, although it was a Catholic coeducational school, I was taught that a lady must shun all men. Naturally, being human, these ideas were not lasting in my mind, but they have left an impression on my personality. I seem to be ill at ease in masculine company probably because I have never been in the presence of men enough to teach me to relax. I am restless and prefer to be out in the open where there is something to do rather than to sit quietly and talk. The nuns have taught me that I should look for my husband in my own religious group. My parents also have conditioned me to choose my mate on the grounds of religious belief, although they are not quite so severe about it.

My family has brought me up to fear punishment if I think seriously of any boy. This has had the effect of making me do on the sly what other girls are allowed to do as a matter of course. They have tried to teach me that there is no man on earth who is good enough for me. This has had a rather bad effect on me because I try to pick out all the faults instead of the good points in every man

I meet. To a lesser extent than my parents I am inclined
to think that I am a little better than the average person.
My parents are very strict about my social life. When I am
at home, I obey them, but when I am away I enjoy life in
a rather moderate fashion when compared with the average person. The reality of the parental discipline is too
overwhelming for me to go against it.

Those who are without adequate sex information should
read books that will give them a sound and complete
grounding in the essential facts.

The following sources are brief, inexpensive, but adequate for most persons. They are likely to be available in
your college library.

Kirkendall: *Understanding Sex* (pamphlet), Science Research
Associates, Chicago, Illinois.
Duvall: *Facts of Life and Love*, The Macmillan Company,
New York.

Above all, before finishing college, both young women
and young men should have sufficient vocabulary and information to begin the education of their own children in
a natural, matter-of-fact way. By the time most children
are three years of age, or a little past, they ask, "Where do
babies come from?" Unless both father and mother can
answer that question honestly and without shame, they are
not ready to train children of their own.

Good sense in dating

A college campus draws all kinds of young people—
those with too rigid moral standards and a few with almost

none at all. In our day of freedom of choice, no rules can make us behave if we wish to do otherwise. Discipline of the emotions and of sex behavior must be self-imposed in the freedom of association given young people on the campus.

In spite of our struggle toward sex equality, standards are still largely in the control of the female sex. While many men have a high regard for the moral code, in general they are less likely to observe it than are girls. In the end they suffer little penalty for violating it, compared with women. In some male circles, violating the moral code may even be considered smart. At no level of society are violations by the girl laughed away. And in case of pregnancy she is entirely to blame in the eyes of both men and women. She must terminate her college career, seek an abortion with all the risk to health and life this means,[1] or face the responsibility and shame of an illegitimate child. The male can and usually does disclaim all responsibility.

We said at the beginning that conventions are for our

[1] In this connection the fact should be mentioned that none of the drugs which have been sold to produce an abortion will do so. Recently a drug has been used on an experimental basis which may cause an abortion, but it is not available to the public. The emotional shock of premarital sexual intercourse often causes menstruation to cease. The traditional drugs taken to produce abortion often bring back menstruation, making the girl think there has been an abortion.

Abortionists often take advantage of the girl's fear that she is pregnant when menstruation is delayed. Reliable authorities estimate that half the abortions among the unmarried involve no pregnancy. In case of fear of pregnancy or actual pregnancy, a girl's only protection is a reliable physician.

protection. In a very real sense sex conventions are for the protection of women. Birth control has not been so well perfected as to set aside this fact of life. Judson T. Landis, family sociologist at the University of California, made a study of veteran couples in college housing while at Michigan State College after the Second World War.

Of the couples who had a child, one-third had wanted and planned for it; another third had practiced birth control but admitted some carelessness; the other third had practiced the best birth-control techniques they knew and had the child anyway.

The college girl will have to learn new ways of protecting herself, particularly if she has had little experience in dating. When the hands stray in dating, it is time to recognize that motives are not purely romantic.

In the new liberty of the college campus a few hold that a girl must pet to be popular and accepted. Bess writes:

> I got off to a bad start here at college. I knew that dating was an absolute "must" in order to become "anyone," but I had never been asked for more than one date by any fellow in high school, and I was afraid the same thing might happen here at college.
>
> I found that if I allowed fellows to go pretty far in petting, I usually ranked high on their dating list. College fellows are not as smooth as they like to appear, so I seldom had trouble putting a stop to things before they got completely out of hand.
>
> Gradually, however, I began to notice that, while I got plenty of dates, they were never for the very special affairs—a fraternity dance or any other big formal. I was usually escorted to a movie, a juke joint, or just out to a

good place to park. These kinds of dates added up to
nothing in the way of general popularity and plenty in
the way of a bad name.

It isn't easy to change your stripes on a small campus
like this, but I've behaved like a saint for several months
now, and the fellows are beginning to get the point. By
the way, I still get dates, too.

The myth that girls must pet to be popular has been
pretty well exploded by studies at Michigan State College
since the war, and one at Cornell University in 1941. At
neither period did more than 4 per cent of college women
feel that there was any truth in this philosophy. Most of
them said it was definitely not true. Very few men felt
differently about it, 77 per cent saying positively "No," 14
per cent being undecided, and only 9 per cent saying
"Yes."

There are ways we may let another know that we really
care without an excess of physical contact. Once a dating
relationship takes on the character of physical intimacy,
there is little chance of exploring the personality on any
other level or of discovering social, intellectual, and other
lasting mutual interests.

In the long run, dating is a selecting ground for a marriage partner. Before they are through college, most
young men and women select a person who has the character, industry, interests, background, and ideals for their
life partner. The long-run values of romance should never
be forgotten if we wish to have a mature view of life and
happiness.

The essence of morality is that we put off immediate

pleasures for the greater benefit which is likely to be gained by waiting.

Nature provides strong sex drives for the sake of reproduction, but is never interested in our happiness. Nature provides for the future of the race, but conventions provide for the future of our individual happiness and well-being.

Practically all college campuses now have a course in marriage preparation. Such courses take one through problems of dating, mate selection, marital adjustment, and parenthood. These offer an opportunity to true up our ideas and fill in blank spaces in our information.

CHAPTER VIII

The Haunting Past

Living with our feelings and fears

We are born to be loved. But somewhere during early childhood some of us missed this important experience. It is hard to get over the damage to personality this causes, for it makes us anxious about life and often brings a sense of guilt out of nowhere to trouble us when we have actually done no wrong.

Many of the emotional and behavior problems of college students do not arise from unhappy incidents in campus life, but are carry-overs from love-starved childhoods. Young people who have difficulty in making friends or who are embarrassingly eager to be liked might well look back at their childhood home environment to discover the source of their problems.

Here are typical examples of young people who have almost become lost souls because of haunting insecurities of the past. They tell how these feelings came about.

KAY: I was a very affectionate child and became starved for affection in my family where I was shunned instead of loved. At first I tried to acquire attention by putting on scenes, pretending I was ill, or exaggerating some slight incident. I soon found, however, that this was useless. If I exaggerated an illness I would be sharply cuffed and given some bad-tasting medicine by my aunt, without a trace of the sympathy and care that I craved. If I put on a temper tantrum I was placed in a dark closet and left to cry myself to quietness. My aunt did not dare place me in a room with an open window at this time, for I would threaten to throw myself out, and deep down in her heart my aunt was afraid I would really do this. Being a child, I was unable to express my need for affection in logical, unemotional ways, when the temper tantrums brought nothing but punishment. I searched desperately for a new technique and gradually built up a thick shell around myself, which became difficult to penetrate.

CHARLES: As a child I felt that my mother did not love me and that she had never wanted me. Family affection was seldom demonstrated, except toward my younger sister, who had a sweet and loving disposition. She became my mother's petted darling, and the household revolved around her. I became intensely jealous and would have nothing to do with her. As she grew older, her demands and vanity increased at my expense. Our personalities were exactly the opposite, and because I was the older, I was forced to give in to her, as older children should. Even my prized playthings were given to her. I began to feel bitter toward her and mother, and even toward life in general, though I did not know then what it was about.

I have always taken myself too seriously, and especially did I develop the habit at this early stage of life. When the folks went to town they had to be gone for a night, and I was left alone on the farm with my brother and sister.

Or, the folks went out for the evening and stayed late, leaving me to put the children to bed and to take care of the lamps. I felt so sorry for myself that I resolved to commit suicide while the folks were gone, and I even thought out a tragic letter I would leave Mother to make her feel sorry for all her neglect. Actual tears would roll down my cheeks as I mentally wrote the note. I had overheard Mother say once that drowning was considered one of the easiest deaths, while anyone drinking carbolic acid suffered untold agonies before dying. So I would use the acid and make Mother still more sorry.

Needless to say, I never attempted it. And there is no danger of my thinking of it now. Of course, the carbolic-acid scheme was most extreme; and I suppose was planned to draw some attention to myself, though if carried out, the attention could not have been personally enjoyed. Therefore, the only pleasure it gave me was the suffering-hero type, derived from thinking about it.

MAY: I have always wanted to belong to someone to whom I mattered supremely, to be assured sympathy, protection, and understanding, no matter what happened. This sentiment has had the capacity of maintaining itself for years in the face of discouraging opposition. I have never found it in my family and am too uncertain of myself to find it outside.

"I'm afraid to make friends with people," Louise says, "unless they take the first acts of friendliness. I always feel that perhaps I'm 'butting in' on something and should not bother people. At other times, through an effort to overcome this feeling of unwantedness, I become overfriendly with the wrong people and find my feelings hurt more."

Explaining why she is this way, she says, "This started at home when I was taught that children should be seen and not heard, and sometimes not seen. I'm sure my parents love me as much as any parents love their children, but being the younger child, I was sensitive to everyone's opinion and found my feelings hurt exceptionally often.

"Memories of being laughed at and made fun of by my older brother forever seem to haunt me, though these are experiences that most little sisters go through, I suppose. I have always been afraid to say what I think or do what I want for fear someone will laugh at me. Always, no matter what I've done, someone has made fun of my efforts and that has caused me to feel that I'm no good at anything."

Thwarted love

The greatest loves of history have been those which were thwarted in their fulfillment by obstacles. Love is like that. Once blocked, it increases to the point of perfection.

When we associate with a person daily, we know he is flesh and blood and subject to all the weakness this means. But when the image becomes only a product of our imagination, it becomes the fulfillment of all our dreams.

Broken loves can heal, and usually do—though sometimes not very quickly. Harry tells of his:

> I had been going with a girl for three years and we had been planning to stick together until I was through college. Something happened right after I came to college, and I never have found out for sure what it was, but she wrote one letter and simply told me that she guessed

she had never really known me until she found out something after I left. She must have meant it, because she got married soon after that to someone I never knew or heard of. For the last six months I haven't known where she is. I guess nobody knows. For a while I just went around in a daze, trying to figure out what it was all about. It was the worst thing that had ever happened to me in all my life, and I haven't forgotten it yet, but I am recovering slowly. It is wearing off slowly but surely because there is nothing I can do about it except to just acknowledge the fact that I've been a sucker or a victim of the consequences of someone's implicating lies. I think I could have done a lot better studying last fall if it hadn't happened.

Jane lets us in on a little of her experience with love. She writes, "Maybe you don't think a girl seventeen can be in love! But believe me I was really in love. For some time my parents had not approved of this friendship. When it became serious they interfered. My entire family disliked this boy friend, his parents, and friends. At the climax of this conflict I left for college. I still find myself daydreaming about this love affair even though logically I know my parents' decision was the right one."

Katie was betrayed by a pal, which made the pill more bitter. She writes, "My third year in college was a kind of turning point. I was going with a fellow at the time and was very proud of the fact that he was what is colloquially termed a 'big shot.' One of my best friends worked very hard in breaking up the match and succeeded. I was working energetically at my job as song queen when this incident took place and I more or less lost faith in human nature."

This problem of broken hearts takes on new angles in college. Many have left a girl or boy friend back home, and before leaving, they pledged to be true forever. Soon they find themselves growing apart, as it is natural to do. Others are separated by the boy's going into military service. There are also summer vacations when separations are necessary.

Many grow apart in interests while both are on the campus. This may be because someone else is more attractive or because of differences in values, morals, or aspirations which come to light with closer associations. It may be a loss of interest on the part of one or both that neither can explain.

There are fair and unfair ways of breaking off. A boy who merely stops calling, when the couple have been more or less steady, lacks courtesy and consideration for others. This method hurts very much. It leaves the unanswered question, "What's wrong with me?"

Another way is to stage a big quarrel in which blame is placed on the other person. This may arise from jealousy, slights, hurts, boredom, or any one of a number of reasons. After all, what is the point to such a fight? Is anyone to blame in most instances, and if they were, what can be done about it?

It is better for both to recognize that there are sensible reasons why the relationship should end, and to end it without rancor. If one still is deeply in love, it will hurt; but it will hurt less than being mean about it or trying to go on with a relationship that can lead only to further trouble.

If we are sensible and fill our lives with interesting activities, there is little reason for moping around too long about a lost love. There is no "one and only" for anyone. There are many more persons who will interest us, and some of them will not need making over like the one we just lost did. And there are many members of the opposite sex who will find us attractive if we see to it that we are interesting and worth while.

In youth it is easy to get back into circulation again, and maybe next time we shall approach love with more maturity and understanding and see it through to a successful marriage.

Tragedy

Sometimes the fears of our past have come through tragedy—death, divorce of parents, a sudden fire, or an accident that hurt us or destroyed part of our familiar world. The damage persists in our emotions beyond the time when one would reasonably expect it to vanish.

Gladys describes the effect of her mother's death on her. It happened during her first year in high school.

> The warmth of an understanding nature had left with the death of my mother. I spent endless nights in that old, lonely house, cringing each time the wind blew for fear of some unknown thing. I was too proud to admit that I was afraid to stay there alone at night. My father and brother were never home from seven until at least ten. I did not feel sorry for myself because of a certain pride that had to be maintained under every circum-

stance. Gradually this grew into an unhappy introversion. I cried easily every time my brother made a catty remark. Because I had no one to tell my troubles to, I lost friends in school. My grade average went from A to C, because I felt that no one cared anyway. I didn't smile at the upperclassmen, as I had previously done, because I was afraid that they would think I was trying to flirt. They soon had the idea that I thought I was better than the others, when in truth I was suffering deeply.

Joanne says:

After my father died, Mother had to work. From the time I was nine years old, I came home from school to straighten the house and start the dinner. As I grew older my duties of housework increased. I had to rush home after school to get the house straightened. I always had time to talk with other children and play a little, but usually I was in the house doing my chores. My work wasn't always awfully good, of course, but when Mother came home from work, tired and faultfinding, my efforts to please were completely ignored or harshly criticized.

I was always rather shy and seriously sensitive to others' opinions, and my feelings were hurt terribly by Mother's peevish attitude. She was never deliberately cruel to me, but she didn't know how her actions affected me.

This situation led to my feeling of good-for-nothingness because usually for my efforts to please, I received nothing in return. This also developed a sort of ambivalent feeling toward her which I hate to admit but know exists.

I've always felt that I don't really know my mother, for I've never talked over my petty troubles with her. She was never around when I felt the need of someone to talk to; and when she did quit work to be with my brother and me, before I came to college and he went into the Army, I couldn't make myself talk with her despite her efforts to draw me out. In fact, I felt she was prying into something that was none of her business when she was only trying to be compatible.

An unsure person is not likely to take the risk of exposing his feelings and getting hurt again.

The bewilderment of death is often a temporarily disorganizing factor in the experience of a young person. The unanswered "Why" often recurs again and again.

This fall my brother died. I did not even know that he had an operation (and even yet I do not fully understand why he had one) until I got a telegram saying that he was dead. This was one of the biggest blows of my life. My brother was big, strong, and healthy. When I last saw him alive, he looked as if he would live to be one hundred instead of twenty-two.

Such matters are inclined to make me ironical. Why must young, healthy people die? Why can't an old or sickly person go in their place? But then sometimes I think that perhaps sickly persons' parents and friends love them as much as they would healthy people. Again, sometimes I often wonder if the dead are not better off, or if God is not taking the good first?

John writes:

My schoolwork was interrupted by the illness and then the death of my father. His death resulted from cancer which proved to be very painful as it lingered on so long before death. I was hard hit by such a shock as a great fellow like my father passing away so slowly. From the physique of a large man to mere skin and bones was more than I could stand, and I lost complete control of myself. It was like moving ahead with no ultimate reason or outcome. Time passed and I realized that my grief was only adding to my mother's and that I must again find myself and work harder than ever before.

Jerry was adopted. Before long, the knowledge of this fact became bitter reality because of the way his sister used it against him.

At a very early age my sister began teasing me about being adopted. At first I paid little attention to this constant teasing, as I did not understand the full meaning of adoption. As I became older it was a common occurrence to be ridiculed about my being born of different parents than she was. Although I no longer believe this, my ears can be seen to twitch when adoption is mentioned in a conversation. I can assure you that this feeling of adoption was not merely something that had a beginning and an ending. It was not that simple. This sense of being different and alone, beginning as it did in my very early childhood, has developed in me a strong feeling of inferiority and insecurity. The two are related, but the difference lies in the fact that "security comes to an individual because of who he is, but inferiority is attained through what he can do." As an insecure child I didn't have a definite place in my family, and I felt unsettled, tense, and restless. It is to this insecure feeling that I can trace the nervousness I possess today. Other characteris-

tics of my insecurity are the fear of attempting anything
that appears on the surface to be too difficult, the desire
to receive praise and rewards after success or accomplishment, and the avoidance of situations that involve competition. I have improved a great deal in the latter instance, but occasionally I find myself rationalizing by
stating that I'm afraid I will be defeated in a race.

What to do?

We are rare and fortunate indeed if we do not have some
haunting emotional pain carried over from the past—pain
that recurs again and again when our memory drifts in certain directions. The problem, now that the damage is done,
is to find a way to feel secure and to satisfy the wishes that
have been thwarted.

If we have lost security in childhood because of our parents' lack of loyalty to us, we may seek it in religion or we
may find it in companionship and affection of those of our
own age group. Ultimately we may find it in a member of
the opposite sex and in love and marriage.

The great handicap is that we feel awkward and afraid
in seeking the friendship and affection of others. We are
afraid to express warmth in our own personalities because
we don't want to be hurt again by its not being returned
when offered.

Actually, most people are warm and friendly. They will
be responsive to our kindness. The world is a much more
friendly place than we have been led to feel it is because of
our unfortunate beginnings.

A change in our own attitudes will gradually come about

if we try to practice getting out of ourselves and taking others into our confidence and trust.

Don't overdo it when someone responds with friendliness. There is always a danger, when we have been left out of the affections of those who have been closest to us, that we will overrespond to friendliness and affection, becoming monopolistic of the attentions of others. By studying our reactions, we can learn to balance our emotions and gradually find a secure place in the group.

We must never forget that no matter how insecure we feel, there are others who are even more so. They need our help and friendliness. We will find ourselves in helping others realize security.

Severing past connections that are painful

Sometimes our pain from damaged emotions follows us because we allow those who inflicted it to continue to dominate our lives. We are reaching the age where this often need not be.

Sometimes a false sense of obligation to parents or false loyalties persist too long. The undemocratic parent never knows when to let go. Accustomed to directing every step in our lives, this type of parent often tries to control us even more rigidly as we approach the age when we should be making most or all decisions for ourselves.

The author had a most interesting summer teaching a group of about two hundred teachers in British Columbia. The family there, particularly in rural sections, is more authoritarian than the family in the United States, with the possible exception of our more isolated mountain sections. Many of these teachers, even though some had been teaching for several years, were still dominated in an unreasonable manner by the wishes and commands of their parents.

They should have long since severed the connection, begun to build their lives around their own interests, and make plans for themselves. False loyalties, a false sense of duty, or fear of what their parents would do if they rebelled kept them from making the break that all young people must make to be free and adult.

With the extremely authoritarian parent, the break may have to be final. The threat to parental authority may lead the domineering parent to say, "Mind me or get out!" Often as not he will later repent and thereafter accept son or daughter as an adult, but until the authority is challenged, he persists in thwarting the wishes of his children.

Olaf lived under the shadow of an authoritarian father and on his first try found it impossible to make the break. He tells his story:

> When I entered the State College, I still lived at home with my father. He frowned on dances, shows, going with girls, parties, etc. He would never let me have the car. He said it was wrong to waste your time in dancing and pleasure seeking. He willingly paid all my college expenses and bought me all the clothes I wanted. He gave me everything except—and this exception is important —money to spend as I desired. As a consequence, I went to very few shows, and had to attend dances on the sly. I was in love with a girl, and lacked money to take her to shows and dances and to make a good impression on her.

My father's attitude irked me. To me it was tyranny. I could see no justice in it. All my companions attended dances, shows, had parties, went with girls, and drove their fathers' cars. But I could only dream of doing these things.

My desire to do as my companions were doing was intense, yet my father's negative attitude was equally strong. I soon began to lie to my father and to take money out of the cash register in his store. This made me a liar and a thief. I abhorred thieves and liars. My opinion of myself was very low—yet I could not help myself. My father soon discovered what I was doing and stopped it. This friction terminated one night in a grand fight, nearly becoming physical as well as verbal, between my father and myself. I dropped out of college and went back home.

It was two years later before I got the courage to tell Dad I would take his domination no longer. I took my stuff and hitchhiked to the western part of the state, where, during the wheat harvest, I was able to earn enough money to pay my tuition in college. I have been earning my own way and am my own boss.

My father has dropped out of my life, for since I defied him he hasn't even written, let alone offered any help.

Even the will to choose is destroyed if the young person is too much overwhelmed by the authority of an elder. The disastrous effect in destroying one's ability to choose and to take the initiative is illustrated by Leona's case.

I still remained completely dominated by my grandmother. Almost every decision I made, and everything I did, was done because my grandmother willed it. I never stayed away from home more than a half hour after school; never brought anyone to the house because it would worry my grandmother. I didn't resent these things. I had never known anything different. I did realize, though, that my grandmother was dominating me so that I had very little will power of my own. Because I was so dependent on my grandmother, I learned to know her every mood and to act accordingly. I learned to obey instantly and without question.

Parental domination may take other specialized forms. The parent may wish only to select a satisfactory mate for us or decide which vocation we should enter. Up to a point, of course, adult judgment may be wise and helpful. One usually knows whether the advice is given to help or whether the parent is trying to realize his own dreams through our marriage or vocation.

If the latter is true, we call it projection. The parent who is most likely to project his wishes in these fields is the one who has failed to achieve his own life goals and wishes us to do it for him. This is unfair, of course, particularly if the goals do not fit our temperament, interests, and capacities.

Here is a case which illustrates this kind of projection:

My name is Mary. I am here studying because as long as I can remember I have wanted to be a missionary. I have found, since coming to college, that I'm not a linguist, and I have very little interest in anthropology. These things have made me analyze my motives. Why do I want to be a missionary when it is increasingly doubtful that I have the aptitudes?

It all goes back to my mother, I am sure. She meant to

be a missionary, but never had the money to go to college. At twenty-five she had to give up these dreams when she married. I know now that she has tried to form my interest so that I may fulfill her dreams. Can I do it? Another year or two in college may give me the answer. But the further I go the less sure I am about it.

Herb writes:

Some way I feel that being a teacher is the most important thing in the world. My mother has always idealized the teaching profession. All four of us children are planning to teach. I think it is because she terminated a successful teaching career to raise a family, and has always missed it.

With the exception of my younger brother, I can't see but what we are as well fitted for this vocation as any other.

Clare writes:

The unfortunate circumstances of my father's life embedded deeply in his mind the desire to see that his children should have the education that he has not had the opportunity to receive. So great was his desire that I get a good education that I felt I was being driven to do something. He was very stern with me about my studies, and he was so strict that I grew to resent his attitude. This feeling became quite evident when I entered the age when activities outside the home and neighborhood began to interest me. As any normal youth does, I longed for the chance to attend the social functions, such as dances, parties of my friends, and to go to shows and other entertainments. My father's youth had lacked the social activ-

ities that seemed so important in my adolescent development. This fact made it hard for him to understand that
certain things in my youth were different than they had
been in his. Our misunderstanding over these circumstances and his seemingly overemphasized strictness in
connection with my education brought about a feeling
almost akin to hatred toward him, although I loved him as
my father and respected him for his clean living and his
determination.

Sometimes the parent who has been highly satisfied with
his lot in life projects, too. Here is the case of a successful
doctor who felt that there was no vocation in the world for
his children but medicine. The children didn't happen to
be made of the same stuff as he, but he refused to recognize
it.

"He insists that I be a nurse," Kitty writes, "and that
Joe, my twin brother, be a doctor. He sent us to school and
insisted that we register in courses leading to these professions. Both of us are primarily interested in athletics
and coaching. I am continuing my work but find that I
have no interest in nursing. My brother tried medicine but
became so disgusted with his college course that he got into
trouble and was expelled from school."

Jerry was forced to be a farmer by being held on the
farm until he was twenty-one. "My father, in his later
years," he says, "developed an absolute obsession that every
one of his eight sons should be farmers. This influenced my
choice only indirectly—that is, in his wishing to force
farming upon me, he made the vocation extremely odious
to me—but nevertheless the fact that he managed to keep

me there from ages sixteen to twenty-one seems to have won me to the cause of agriculture or something to that effect. I really believe that back of it all was a fear that by living in town and going to high school the family was becoming foppish, lightheaded, and wishing to live beyond their means."

Sometimes it is not the parents but some other person who is frustrating our growth toward maturity. One of the privileges of maturity is that we make up our own minds about issues that concern us. Advice should never be ignored, but if we are to acquire adulthood, we have to assert the right to choose for ourselves. For some of us, this is the only road to peace.

CHAPTER IX

There's a Job in Your Future

Young people today realize that college can make a big difference when it comes to finding a job. Fifty years ago when most people didn't get beyond the eighth grade, the high-school graduate had a big advantage in competition for the better jobs. Today nearly everyone attends high school as a matter of course, and college or other special vocational training is almost necessary for getting ahead vocationally.

Of course, everyone who enters college doesn't do so for vocational reasons. Many young people just seem to drift into college for no special reason. As one boy put it, "After high school, I had no idea what to do, so I came to college." Others come because of their parents' wishes and ambitions for them. A few merely want to put off the inevitable day when they must strike out on their own, and still others hope that their college classes and activities will suggest interesting vocational possibilities.

Regardless of why we decided to come, most of us realize that college can make a big dollars-and-cents difference in terms of the jobs that await us in the years ahead.

Pinning ourselves down

For those who have always known where they were headed, as well as for those who remain undecided, college represents the logical time for pinning ourselves down on the matter of a vocational choice. This does not mean that a person must or even should make an irrevocable decision about a specific job. It does mean, however, that at some time during our college years we are both old enough, wise enough, and experienced enough to forget a lot of our impossibly romantic childhood ambitions and knuckle down to the serious business of deciding at least the general field for which we are the most suited. Lynn tells of this fact in her autobiography. She writes:

> I have always planned to be an interior decorator. I imagined myself dashing around in swank apartments and fabulous homes telling people where they should put this and that, the colors they should use, and the furniture they should have. In my daydreams I was always the unconventional, temperamental artist whom everyone admired.
>
> The funny thing is I'm not really very artistic. Since I've been in college, I've discovered that the interior decorator isn't just a self-styled expert, but a well-trained planner with years of art courses and special training behind him. I've found that most graduates in this field must spend years in doing such menial jobs as hanging drapes, selling furniture, and so on before any company is interested in them as interior decorators.
>
> I've decided that my ambitions were more than a little farfetched. Now I'm ready to consider the things I really

can do well and begin to think more realistically about a future vocation.

Where does college come in?

Colleges offer plenty of assistance to those interested in making up their minds about vocational plans.

Most colleges, for example, have some kind of advisory system in which students have the opportunity to talk over their plans (or their lack of plans) with a faculty member or some especially trained counselor. The student who is pretty certain about his vocational plans is helped in selecting courses that lead in the right direction. The student who has no idea about what he wants or where he is headed is given special kinds of assistance. Sometimes he is urged to sample several areas by taking a well-rounded program of courses. Frequently he is urged to attend special meetings and exhibits where the opportunities and assets of various vocations are discussed. But one of the most important services the college or university has to offer is its testing setup. Let us look at this in greater detail.

One of the basic causes of vocational uncertainty and indecision is the fact that many young people do not know what their real interests and aptitudes are. The testing service makes it possible for an individual to gain a clearer picture of his own interests and abilities and also to see what they mean as far as jobs are concerned. The tests generally do more than indicate a general ability; they also point up one's temperamental suitability. Jess, for example, had a way of talking that made people listen. She sounded sincere and sympathetic and spoke with an air of self-assurance which attracted confidence and respect. Everyone felt certain that if Jess became some kind of salesperson, she was sure of tremendous success. Still, she disliked the idea of selling in spite of the financial rewards. Tests and counseling indicated that while her manner was very convincing, Jess really dreaded contacts with new people. She liked to remain among friends and familiar faces.

The outgrowth of this examination of herself led Jess to consider radio work rather than conventional selling. After several years of training, she became a successful announcer for a well-known broadcasting company. Now she admits, "I don't mind selling things to people. I just don't want to watch their faces while I'm doing it."

Counselors are very careful not to *tell* an individual what job he should go into. The tests are not crystal balls. They can tell something of our native ability and our interests, but they cannot assure us of success in any particular position. The more general and diversified one's abilities, the fewer specific answers these tests can give. In any case, there are other factors in addition to ability and interest which will have a part in determining whether we shall ever succeed at any particular job. Our drive is one of the most important of these factors.

Drive versus talent

The individual for whom everything seems to come easily may just drift along and make less of his ability than he should. Talent without industry and strength of purpose is of little value. All of us have known of others with only average ability who have achieved outstanding success by application and industry. Whether or not we succeed at our chosen vocation depends not alone upon the talents nature gave us and upon our training but also upon our will to make the most of whatever talents we possess.

Job availability

Another factor in determining whether or not we shall succeed in the vocation of our choice is the principle of supply and demand. When a new field opens up, there is generally a big demand for people to fill the jobs. Even those with relatively little talent or training can often succeed. Later, when more people begin to train for the new field, employers have more applicants among whom to choose. They can afford to be more discriminating.

When college students begin to think seriously about the job in their future, they should do more than consider their own interests and aptitudes; they should also look at the general job situation and ask themselves such questions as these:

1. Is there really a demand for people in the occupation I hope to enter?
2. Will this demand still exist by the time I have finished my education?
3. Will I be as well qualified for employment in my chosen field as are those who are currently being employed there?
4. Is there a future in the occupation of my choice, or will it, like glass blowing and blacksmithing, soon be a thing of the past?

Being realistic about our own abilities and interests and the demands of the field we hope to enter may take a little of the romance out of our dreams and ambitions, but it can save us from disappointment, as well as bankruptcy, in the years ahead.

Making the decision

Many college students would be willing to drift along taking courses in this and that, putting off from one semester to the next their decision about a vocational goal. College administrators know this and have instituted a rule whereby all students must, by a certain time, declare a major—in other words, state a particular course of study upon which they intend to concentrate.

In some schools and in some fields in most schools, freshmen are expected to declare a major at the very beginning. Other schools do not permit it until the student reaches the beginning of the sophomore or junior year. But whenever it comes, for many it comes too soon. Declaring a major is tentatively declaring one's life objective and plans.

The student is never bound to his first choice. If, after additional experience or thought, he decides to change his major, he is permitted to do so. It is not unusual to be undecided about a major. In fact, it is a very common experience. A few years ago one of my graduate students, Charles Nelson, studied the number of times college young people change majors. He found that a very high proportion changed majors at least once during their college years—and some more than once. One should not switch a major merely because he does not like a particular course or a particular professor. On the other hand, if he finds that his interests are much more vital in a field other than the one he is in, he should not be embarrassed to change. A part of the value of college is that it gives us a chance to appraise ourselves and to do some backtracking and starting over if we find it necessary to our success and happiness. But there is a big advantage in thinking it over seriously and trying to make the first choice a lasting one. Each field has its special requirements. Much time and effort are wasted in transferring from one major to another unless the fields are closely related.

Vocational quandaries

Changing our majors, of course, is only an indication that we are still unsure of our vocational interests and aptitudes. Most of us have gone through many changing vocational-interest stages. Most little girls, for example, want to be nurses, while their brothers dream of cowpunching or fire fighting. A little later, the girl may want to be an actress, while the boy is interested in aviation or exploring.

I once asked a college class to write a brief note indicating the number of times they had changed their vocations and what these changes had been. Here are some of their reactions to the question:

GIRLS:

> I have changed my mind quite a few times, but I don't know whether it was just a fad or really a desire to be these things. I wanted to be an aviatrix once, but it would

cost too much money, so I gave that up. Once I wanted to be a nurse, but my sisters talked me out of that. I've wanted to be a teacher for a long time—since I was in the eighth grade.

I've changed six times. At first I wanted to be a nurse. Quite a few of the girls who graduated with me decided to go into nurses' training. They were very enthusiastic about it. My sister and my family discouraged that. I wanted to be a schoolteacher when I was about twelve and, then later, a movie star.

At ten I wanted to be a bookkeeper; at about fifteen or sixteen I wanted to be a math teacher—this was because I liked my high-school math so well; at seventeen I decided to take a commercial course since I could not major in math, and then my father suggested that it would be more worth while to take commerce for stenographic purposes; at nineteen I decided I wanted to teach commerce.

I once considered majoring in clothing and design in hopes that I'd eventually be a style specialist, but the openings for such a position require so much experience and the cost of preparation is so great that I changed to education which offered sooner returns. I also thought of dietetics but my sister, who is a nurse, dissuaded me. As a child I had splurges of wanting to be a great singer, actress, and missionary.

First, I wished to be a nurse when quite small, but this was just an idea. Then I wished to be a secretary. Since giving this up, I have decided on the teaching vocation.

Four times I've changed. Usually, after deciding on a vocation, I have had some experience in the chosen field which convinced me that I did not like it. On the last one, I had the experience first and chose afterward.

BOYS:

I've changed three times—once I made up my mind to be an M.D. (age eleven). Then I decided to be an engineer (age fourteen). I now believe that I should like to be an M.D. and a psychiatrist, but I will not decide until I have made a thorough investigation of my abilities and interests in the vocation.

I've changed many times. It has been very difficult for me to decide this question. Lack of training has kept me from entering some fields. It has been a constant problem to know what to enter. Choices have ranged from a chemist to a psychologist, and from a captain of industry to a salesman. But the general aim has been toward business. If it were not for lack of funds for further education, necessity of earning a living, and a few other minor things, I would go on now and study to be a vocational director. I am very interested in this field and believe it to be one of great opportunity—this is my second choice. I will have to accept it as a hobby.

I have decided upon many vocations before arriving at this one. I have talent in music, art, and mechanics, so I naturally felt a desire for a vocation in all of these fields. The vocation I chose combines art and mechanics. Music can be taken up as a hobby.

The longer I attend school, the less I know as to what I want to do.

At the age of six I wanted to be a painter. At the age of ten a trader and trapper. By the time I was fifteen I was torn between the desire to be an electrician, for which I had considerable aptitude, and that of being a piano player, at least equal to Paderewski, for which profession I had no talent whatsoever and less opportunity of instruction.

The thought of bringing any woman out to live amid the dreariness and drudgery of farm life made me dread agriculture as a vocation, unless one could be a "gentleman" farmer. I still want to do some writing. I believe that this is because of a desire for self-assertion and recognition to compensate for the feeling that the vocation of farming sets up the idea in the minds of other people that "one is a farmer because he cannot be anything else. . . ."

If we could follow these same young people on through college and even after college, we would find that some of them are still not decided or not quite satisfied with the choices they made.

At times we have to decide on the basis of opportunities that open for us. Sometimes interests change with experience; the thing that looks so inviting before we get into it often proves to be quite boresome to us. It is not always possible for us to have a long look at this job business, and it is seldom too late to experiment and to change. That is normal in American society. Some people even change at middle age and yet make a career—a distinguished career—for themselves.

Of this much we are certain: it is better to change than to suffer boredom and frustration from a job that is entirely unpleasant to us. This does not mean that any vocational field we choose will not have a certain amount of boredom and routine grind in it.

Vocational education versus vocational training

A few years ago when jobs were very scarce, the American Youth Commission, after studying the employment experiences of young people and their work opportunities, concluded that specific vocational training is much less necessary in the modern world than a broad understanding of vocational opportunities. They concluded, therefore, that vocational education in the broad sense is much more important for the average young person than training for a specific vocation as such.

In the broadest sense, college offers vocational education which prepares one to adapt to many work situations. It broadens his horizons of the variety of work situations; it acquaints him with professional people and specialists who put him in touch with work situations; it often provides him with an introduction to talent scouts from various industries who visit the campuses each spring looking for talent via the professors.

It is not too early, at the beginning of a college career, to realize that the impression one makes on his professors as a student is likely to have a decided bearing on the place he finds in the work world immediately upon graduation. Those who go into professional fields or government employment must have recommendations to obtain positions. Professors' recommendations follow the young graduate for many years after he is out in the field. Whether or not they can conscientiously back a person as one who is industrious, capable, and conscientious will have a great deal to do with his success.

Many young people entering college do not realize this fact, but it is an important one, as any professional person would advise. They got their start by certain professors' backing them for a job and helping them get a better one if they succeeded on their first job.

In the United States, vocational climbing is largely a matter of moving from the first job to a better one on the basis of recommendations given by professors and later on by employers.

When we sum it all up then, we must recognize that college is a very important preparation for our entry to the work world, and it will give us an advantage in competition with those who do not go to college. In Chapter XVI we shall discuss the financial rewards of education.

CHAPTER X

Shall I Dream or Do?

The importance of action

Inaction is often paralyzing; action relieves us and sets us free. Since James and Lange, two famous psychologists, stated their theories of emotions, there has been much argument about the relationship between action and emotion.

Some psychologist said we run because we are afraid; these men argued that we are afraid because we run. We need not settle the argument here. We do know that there is a relationship between fear, and our other emotions, and action.

When a house is on fire, a rather frail person may get a huge piece of furniture out singlehanded. That is putting fear into action. Others who hesitate and can't get going become so overcome with fear that someone has to lead them out of the house so others can work.

The simple physiological process is this: When an object of fear comes in our path—like the sudden outbreak of fire or a snake in the road—our adrenal glands shoot their hormones into the blood stream to prepare us for the fight. Our stomach slows down; the flow of blood speeds up in our fighting muscles; blood sugars are released from our liver to give us strength. We are supermen—if we act! If we fail to act, we are soon overcome by the excess energy that nature has wasted on us.

It is surprising how many times our indecision, our emotional upsets, our feelings of despair can be banished if we act instead of brood. Action of almost any type helps to relieve the tensions produced by frustration and indecision. Temper tantrums and bursts of anger and tears will do the job, but there are other more constructive and socially approved means to express ourselves in finding relief.

Play and work are healthy outlets

Play is an excellent means of working off excess energy. All of us need play and diversion. The busier we are, the more we need the relief of play.

Jeff, for example, writes of using tennis to work off anger he was unable to display openly.

"No one ever argued in our family; it just wasn't done. 'If you feel that you have been mistreated,' my father used to say, 'then let's talk it over quietly and reach an understanding like gentlemen.' His idea was okay, and it did help to get misunderstanding straightened out with a minimum of hard feelings. But even after talking things over, the feeling of anger and frustration was hard to shake off. Still, you can't yell at a person like Dad, who has been decent and completely reasonable. So I used to work off my steam by batting a tennis ball against the side of our house, sometimes for half an hour at a time."

Keep a hobby and keep play in your life through college. If you have not learned to play, you must in order to lead a balanced and happy life. Play is an outlet through which we may act. It is physically restful, relieves tensions, and acts as a safety valve for our emotions. Play, too, is one of the best ways man has invented for getting close to others and sharing with them. We take down our guards in happy play and let others in.

Work, too, is an effective outlet for energy. Work is easier than brooding. The unhappiest students I know are those who sit around and brood about an English theme or algebra problem. Instead of getting into the fight, they let their ductless glands pile up the energy without using it. Act!

One summer I went to a town to teach an extension course and no pupils showed up. The principal who had scheduled the course—unwisely, it seemed, since no one was interested in it—was very embarrassed. He had set out a whole roomful of chairs. A few minutes after the class hour had arrived, and while we waited, he began to shove all these chairs, except a half dozen in the first row, back into the corner in a tight group. "It will look better this way," he explained, "if we are going to have only a few students."

When no one came, and we were laughing together about it, he explained why he had moved the chairs. He said, "I was getting a headache when I saw how things were turning out. It was extremely embarrassing not to have this course materialize. I have a tendency to get ulcers. When my emotions begin to disturb me, I find it relieves me to do something, so I shoved the chairs back. I felt a lot better after I started to do something."

It was a very simple cure for his momentary frustration and defeat. When you get to brooding over an assignment or other problems, pull the books off the shelf and pitch into it with all your might and see how quickly anxiety will vanish.

Pitching into hard work, whether mental or physical, not only relieves frustration but, better yet, it gets things done. An author does not sit around gawking at the typewriter or tape recorder. Ideas come as he begins to act. Better a dozen false starts which go into the wastebasket than no start at all. Action brings both relief and results.

The behavioristic psychologists discovered that all thinking is talking to ourselves. When we think, our throat muscles move as we try to juggle the word symbols which we use for thinking, much as a stonemason shifts the stones around to make them fit their place.

If you must walk about the room to think, then walk about. If you must take the pen and start to scribble, or the typewriter and start to pound the keys, do it; the way to get going is to act.

If we can apply this rule to ourselves, learning to come to grips with problems and assignments quickly and decisively, many of our moods and painful indecisions will vanish; and we shall add positive attributes to our personalities.

Some people react to hardships and frustrations, not by turning outward—looking for interests and activities outside themselves—but by escaping to a world within themselves.

Introversion as an escape

Introversion—the tendency to withdraw into ourselves—is more natural for some than for others. It becomes an especially handy device for those who have been hurt by their fellows. Unfortunately, the more we withdraw the more we are concerned about ourselves and our problems, and the less about others and the way they feel.

We can become so introspective that we soon resemble a great Italian scientist who was a visiting lecturer in an American university. He carried a thermometer about with him all the time. Whenever he felt a little flush, pain, or chill, he took his temperature. This had become such an obsession with him that he often took it several times a day. He never enjoyed his robust health.

Much of our introspection is about as useless as it is foolish. No one is going to eat us up if we trust ourselves to the good will of others.

Yet there are many reasons for withdrawal, as the accounts of students show.

Here is Gloria, disillusioned because others have not always respected her ideals. She withdraws to protect them.

"I am an introvert," she writes, "a tender-minded individual. Perhaps the reason back of this lies in my disillusionment. I had certain idealistic ideas which I thought people should be glad to recognize. They didn't. This bitter and disappointing experience left such a wound that

I'm afraid I will again become irritated if I accept leadership."

Too much domination and a lack of trust by an elder
drove Teresa into her shell, where self, music, and solitude
are her companions.

Although my aunt financed my business training, she
made any gratitude that I showed unbearable by her
absolute dominance. Positive that I was taking the down-
ward path along with the rest of the modern generation,
she allowed me no normal recreation at home or expres-
sion of views for fear it would lead to "the worst." And so
I gradually developed a shell into which not even my
parents dared enter. I found solace in my music, solitude,
and a few true friends. This shell has created a sense of
insufficiency and a daydream of some day becoming important.

Thelma suffered from differential treatment and attention by her aunt.

During this time came the beginnings of an inferiority
complex that became a phobia to me. To begin with, I
was seldom as well dressed as my cousin. Since my aunt
looked upon the family as decidedly a charity case, she saw
no reason for dressing me as well as her own daughter.
Secondly, the aunt—although a kind woman in many
respects—couldn't refrain from telling other people just
how kind she was in caring for her brother-in-law's children. To an extremely self-conscious child it was horribly
embarrassing to hear myself discussed to everyone on the

streets or in homes. It made the situation worse that my aunt was an ignorant, tactless woman. My only refuge was to retire further within myself. So I developed more surely into an introvert personality and became classed as a "queer child."

Introversion not a disease

It is only when we get so far from reality that we hate to recognize it, or fail to cope with it, that introversion becomes abnormal.

It is easy to see that many have had to use it as the only way of protecting their personalities from slights and hurts. Some change considerably when the conditions that hurt them have been removed. For all of us, college offers an opportunity to turn over a new leaf, to begin to trust people and share more freely with them.

This does not mean that we must all become jovial extroverts, hail fellows well met. That role is for politicians and social climbers. Most of us can never play it and should never try. We can get out of ourselves without this.

We all need to share confidences—some with one or a few, others with many. If we haven't been doing it, the time to begin is now. Friendliness brings friendliness in return.

College life offers great opportunities for those of us with introvertive tendencies to correct and compensate for our fears and hurts. Scholastic achievement requires a certain amount of introversion. Study offers an opportunity to turn away from self-absorption to problems external to ourselves, and it thereby takes us in the direction of creative usefulness.

Great talents have appeared in introverted persons who by their cultivation of modest abilities made outstanding contributions to invention and abstract knowledge.

CHAPTER XI

Conflicts, Glands, and Guilt

The meanness within us

In their college autobiographies young people tell of their struggles with bad tempers and mean dispositions. They know that success from here on is going to be determined by the extent to which they are able to master these deficiencies and put on a pleasant front in dealing with others.

Here are a couple of boys who tell of their struggles with bad temper:

RONALD: One of my characteristics is my temper. As a rule, my outward temper is quite cool and unmoved, even though I do get so annoyed and irritated that I could easily commit murder. I have an uncanny faculty for keeping my excessive, hot-blooded temper well under control even though irritated to the utmost. One of the things that arouses my ire is the inconsideration of other people. Although they are congenial and friendly, they have no respect for the rights of others. As an example, I shall use my rooming house. Our room is the largest, and the other fellows of the house entertain their friends in our room, sleep and study there, giving no consideration to our wants or our desires whatever. Sometimes my blood fairly boils, but as yet I have kept my temper well under control. Eventually, however, my temper will break loose and then my rights will be recognized, even though I use my meager physical power.

ELTON: Among my faults which have been hard to overcome are my sensitiveness and my bad temper. The latter is usually the result of the former. I don't like to be kidded, and when people know it, they try to make me lose my temper. They usually succeed. This is probably the result of my self-consciousness in regard to my accent. As a child I was petted and spoiled because I was the youngest child, and it has been difficult for me to understand why I shouldn't always have my own way.

Moodiness

Some people get moody and some blue and despondent. Others have the habit of self-pity.

Psychologists tell us we all tend to go through a cycle of moodiness. It may hit some every two weeks or so, some every four or five. Some of us even have a daily mood cycle, feeling lighthearted and gay when we awake in the morning but dull and morose before the day is through; some can't get going before noon and are just getting warmed up about ten-thirty at night. (These moods are entirely aside from the tenseness or depression women often feel immediately preceding menstruation.)

If we study our moods and chart them for a while, we may be able to anticipate our dark times, particularly if we are the kind who sink awfully low when we are in a mood.

Boys more often confess to their troubles over temper; girls over moodiness.

"I am the introvert type," Kay says. "I spend much time daydreaming about my ambitions and planning to carry them out but never get any place with them. I am characterized by changing moods. I do not carry them to extreme, but they are very noticeable, even to a stranger."

Judy writes:

> My fluctuation of moods is noticeable at times—at least to my friends. I know that at times I am too moody, but I don't know why. I come to school in the morning in a fairly cheerful mood, and then all of a sudden or gradually I become moody and rather irritable. Usually my intimate friends just leave me alone when I am that way and let me "come out of it" by myself. I am deeply moved by sorrow or sad happenings, but this is not usually the cause of my moodiness. The only explanation I can give for most of the moodiness is perhaps my feelings are too easily hurt or that I imagine that things about me are going on behind my back. I have always tried to convince myself that my feelings are not so vulnerable and that I am not easily hurt.

Knowing our mood cycles helps us to plan our lives somewhat more efficiently. People with particularly strong moods of bitterness or self-pity usually find it better to steer clear of conflict situations during their depressed period. Extreme moodiness can be a sign of serious problems that need the attention of a physician.

Moods, even sad ones, are not always undesirable, as the following sketch indicates:

I wouldn't trade my Friday-night depressions for a dozen more happy hours a week. I've grown much too attached to them. Mother and Dad used to worry about my almost-weekly periods of blueness and self-pity, but now I think even they are reconciled to their "queer daughter."

Friday evenings, after dinner, when most students are celebrating the end of classes till Monday morning, I curl up in a big chair and wait for "Mr. Blues." (I think it's more habit now than actual moodiness.) But anyway, Mr. Blues seldom fails me. With a coke, potato chips, and soft record music (*Isle of the Dead* or the *Unfinished Symphony*) I'm all prepared for an hour or so of real down-right unhappiness.

About a year ago, while I was still in high school, I discovered that writing my unhappy thoughts down in poetry made them even better. One poem I considered so good that I sent it in to a poetry magazine. They published it; I've been profiting financially by my mood sessions (Dad calls them the "graveyard shift") as well as enjoying them, ever since.

Guilt

Guilt is a hard thing to live with. It haunts us in the night; it brings terror in our times of exhaustion and fear. In the crowd we may be courageous and daring and defy our conscience, but in the night it is our master.

Conscience was long considered to be the voice of God speaking to us. Actually, it is a man-made thing. It is the voice of guilt that speaks when we violate standards that our families and society have implanted deep within us.

It is our self-critical self that tells us we are wrong, that we are without excuse.

One of the greatest struggles of man with conscience ever portrayed is that by Hawthorne in *The Scarlet Letter*. The Reverend Dimmesdale literally fades away and dies over the period of a few years from the torment of a secret, gnawing guilty conscience.

The Russian novelist Feodor Dostoevski in his great psychological novel, *Crime and Punishment,* depicts a young man gripped by a guilty conscience almost to the point of madness. He trapped himself under the shrewd eyes of a detective who understood the workings of the guilty heart.

From childhood we have been taught certain codes of conduct. They are our guides to live by. Some are not important to us because they have not been deeply implanted. Some are so deep within us that their violation will torment us in our waking hours and in our dreams. Other people may disregard these standards, but when we do, we have double-crossed ourselves, and this is torment.

This is where the real problems of sex delinquency center. Physically, sex is normal and natural. In many societies premarital sexual relations are condoned. Where this is so, there is no psychological problem.

But within our codes, chastity is the social rule under which most of us grew up. It is in our morals and our religion. It is woven into the warp and woof of our personalities as few if any other codes are.

Guilt in this area can bring the worst of shock and torment and be the basis of nervous breakdowns.

Worries about our past missteps

Sex ventures and experiments during childhood or early adolescence are not abnormal. Exploring is, in fact, quite normal behavior.

Masturbation, which for some brings much guilt, is normal during the period of puberty, and often persists to some degree until marriage. It does no physical or mental damage aside from the guilt which may have resulted from false teaching. It does not unfit one for marriage.

The persistent belief that it leads to mental disease or nervousness is purely a myth in which medical science takes no stock. Students of sexology believe that masturbation is almost universal at some period in childhood or youth, particularly for the boy.

The only danger in it is that if persisted in to excess, it tends to isolate one from normal heterosexual activities which provide a normal outlet for sex feelings prior to marriage and which lead to a regular heterosexual life after marriage.

Our sibling jealousies

Most of us have brothers and sisters. Generally this is better than having none. We may have lived under their shadows or they under ours. Life cannot be the same for us as it would have been had they not existed.

Sociologist Jesse Bernard has made an extensive study of the research on sibling rivalries and the effect on per-

sonality of being the oldest, youngest, and in-between.
She concludes: [1]

> If, standing on a crowded street corner, we could see
> all the adults about us in terms of their sib relationships,
> we would see not the seemingly independent, self-
> resourceful individuals who pass before us, but rebellious
> little sisters fighting against parental discrimination, re-
> sentful little brothers hating older sisters whose superi-
> ority in age and maturity frustrated their male egos, jeal-
> ous older sisters resenting the attention bestowed on
> little sisters, sisters of all ages envying the privileges of
> brothers of all ages. Most of us, on becoming closely ac-
> quainted with men and women of apparent maturity,
> have found that in certain aspects of their personalities
> they are still much under the influence of brother or sister,
> still smarting under childhood patterns. It does not matter
> that they are now successful in their own right; they must
> still convince brother or sister of their success. One man's
> whole life is spent in achieving goals which his sister
> unconsciously set for him years ago; he must prove to her
> that he can do it. One woman's life is shattered because of
> her ambivalent attitude of hatred and love for a brother
> who dominated her childhood.

If we probe our past even superficially, we shall see
where we fitted into the pattern of brother and sister relationships. What has it done to us? How can we compensate for it, if at all?

Sometimes it is easy to see what to do. If we have been
overshadowed all our life by an older brother and his

[1] *American Family Behavior*, p. 312, Harper & Brothers, New York,
1942.

school or athletic record, we should by all means go to another school where we can live without having the records compared. It is not always that simple, of course.

Here a girl tells what she helped make of her brother Jimmy under her parents' direction. She is aware of why Jimmy is what he is. But has Jimmy awakened yet?

Although honesty, loyalty, truthfulness, cleanliness, and good manners were stressed by my parents, the fact that I was responsible for Jimmy seemed to me to be the first law. Mother would look into my eyes and say, "Jane, I trust you to see that nothing happens to Jimmy." Nothing did if I was around. Because Jimmy was small for his age, and I was unusually tall and well-built for mine, I fought his battles for him, cried when he was spanked. I did all his work for him in school, I made excuses for him—in fact, I tried to assume more than my share of the responsibility. For myself I do not regret the responsibility Mother placed on my shoulders. For Jimmy, I do. It was a great misfortune for him and also Mother and Daddy. He floated through his little-boy days too easily and now he is having a tougher time. Since high school, he has had to assume the responsibility for his actions. He has to do his own schoolwork and take the blame for his conduct, whereas I had always done it. Life has always been a dream, and he is having a difficult time to adjust himself to the world from which we did our best to shield him.

Jo lived under the shadow of her brother. "Michael was two years older than I," she explains. "He teased me endlessly. Because of my temperament, I refused to give in to his teasing and arguing; this resulted in much unhappiness in my family. I took things too seriously which was unfortunate for I became bitter. This affected my relationships with my friends outside the family."

Gregory was reared by his sisters. A junior in college, he still can't tolerate the thought of dating a girl. Here is why:

> I have never had a "date" with any girl in my life. This may seem peculiar and class me as something less than normal, one who is contrary to the laws of nature. It may be so, but I think I can easily explain why my behavior is this way. My father died when I was six years old and left me with a mother and four sisters. I grew up with girls and before I was very old, I vowed if all girls were like my sisters, I did not want anything to do with them. I think that the only thing that can change this emotional status is to get out of this community and out of the midst of my family. This will force me to find some outlet for my emotions.

Studies of delinquency and crime show that the oldest child is the most often involved. It may be that he gets this way from playing the hero for the younger children. It may be, too, that he keeps the younger children from getting away with things he got away with, because he is a sort of parent who watches them when adults are not around. Or it may be that he feels he has to venture outside the family and pave the way. The younger children follow the path he has broken to the outside and never develop his toughness.

There is also the possibility that he may more often feel the need to rebel. Parents learned to be parents when he came into their home. Usually parents are more demanding of the first one, and he is frustrated more. Having learned how to be parents at his expense, they are more able to let the younger children grow up naturally.

We usually think of the youngest child as being the spoiled baby who has been coddled so much he has a hard time fitting into the cold world outside. He is more likely to be submissive. The older child, who by virtue of greater physical strength has been boss, tends to be domineering.

There is much more to it, of course. An attractive child may get so much attention from family, friends, and guests as to become the object of envy for the other children, regardless of their age. This child may be happy and well-adjusted, while the others are spoiled in disposition by the situation of unsuccessful rivalry.

These are the kinds of chances that life brings to all. We are formed by them.

What to do?

Overrepressions often have serious effects on personality. This was first suggested by Freud, who made a great contribution to psychology by describing the nature and functions of the subconscious mind. Our mind is like an iceberg—four-fifths submerged.

Unpleasant experiences, like anger and jealousy, that we dare not show, are filed in the subconscious. If they are associated with very distasteful emotions, they often simmer and boil until they become like a volcano. We need to let off steam.

An old proverb says, "An honest confession is good for the soul." Many religious systems have used the confession technique as a device for ridding men and women of their suppressed emotions, guilt, and fears. Among early Methodists it was the weekly class meeting where, in a small group a member would get up and tell how he had fared. If he seemed to be covering up, the class leader probed him with leading questions until he came clean. The Catholic Church still employs the confessional to help its parishioners relieve themselves of guilt.

In these days, when so many question religion, other organizations have had to be substituted for them. Alcoholics Anonymous employs the confessional and testimony meeting of the old-fashioned Methodists as a means of freeing men from guilt and giving them strength to combat temptation.

Psychiatry is now a highly paid profession. The couch of the psychiatrist has become the confessional of the sophisticated and prosperous. Psychological clinics are on the increase, and even the quack who hangs out his shingle as a psychological counselor can get a clientele. Yet nervous breakdowns increase, and the psychiatric wards of hospitals and the hospitals for the mentally ill are always crowded. There are more mental patients in hospitals than there are patients for all forms of physical illness. In fact, many physical illnesses so-called are psychologically induced.

Studies of animals show that they, too, can be neurotic

and suffer mental breakdowns by having too many problems to solve, by being irritated too often by situations which bring them pain and unhappiness.

Expressing our unhappiness, our hostilities and frustrations is essential to good physical and mental health. Our family and community could not, of course, allow us to express all of them directly through fighting, arguing, or temper tantrums. Talking out our anger, writing down our gripes, blowing off steam in discussions, hard work, and hard play are ways of finding relief without losing friends.

Confession is often needed. It may be to a friend, a confidant, a parent, a trusted teacher, a minister, or a member of the college counseling staff. We need not shut ourselves in, for there is always a sympathetic ear to listen if we will but open up.

We can often help ourselves by helping others who are in more trouble than we. Many make their first forward steps when they begin to try to do things for others. During the war it was discovered that the best cure for the neurotic soldier, when he was over the first stage of recovery, was to have him help and counsel those who were in worse condition than he.

We have to come to terms with ourselves. We are not someone else, no matter how much we wish we were. Sometimes we live so in awe of a parent or some other person who has been our hero that we belittle ourselves and fail to push ahead to achieve. If we begin making the most of what we have, we shall soon be proud of who we are and not need to envy or secretly worship others.

We must find avenues where we can succeed and be content to be our best there. Let others excel in their lines of superior ability. If we can achieve, we need not envy others and retaliate with jealousy and ill nature. No two people can be alike. People will like us for what we are, if we will but like ourselves and act it.

CHAPTER XII

Escaping or Going Places

Some young people are so full of complexes that they are motivated not so much by reason as by a desire to escape from, or to compensate for, certain frustrations. We have already indicated that compensation is a powerful factor in human achievement. There is no mistaking that. Those who suffer from a deep sense of inferiority do have to fight for recognition by means of various compensative devices or give up in despair.

As we approach maturity, however, it is well to analyze our goals and objectives, particularly if we have extremely strong drives, to see whether we are carrying them in a direction that is practical and realizable. For example, a girl with a severe inferiority complex may be determined to settle for nothing less than a career on the stage. This is all right, providing she has the talent to realize such ambitions. If not, perhaps she should settle for a less distant goal and try to be happy with an achievement within the range of her talents.

Much defeat and frustration lie ahead for those who are unwilling to face their limitations as well as their strong points. To face these limitations is to be realistic about

one's future and to plan for a future which is within reach.
Only a genius can afford to hitch his wagon to a star. For
most of us, to aim at a distant mountain top is high enough.
One should never be satisfied with less than he is capable
of. But if one is capable of only average achievement, he
should take this into account in his plans and in his
training.

In this chapter I am going to present a case of a young
woman, a real case except for the fictitious name I have
attached to her. I call this girl Dora Dover. She was in one
of my classes and wrote this account of her personality development and future plans. As the case is told, let us analyze it and see whether she is escaping from something or
actually going places. When Dora wrote this account, she
was seventeen years of age and a sophomore.

My present community is a college campus, a solid
square mile of classrooms, activity centers, organizations,
and what have you. But for me, it includes only the dormitory, the classrooms, and the library.

A typical day would picture me rising about 6:30 A.M.,
taking a shower, listening to the newscast while dressing
and doing my room work, going down to breakfast silently to plan my work for the day, returning to my room
to brush up assignments, then reading all day or going
to classes, stopping only for the news broadcast, the news-
papers, lunch at noon, and dinner at night. Occasionally,
I help some girl with her English theme. At 10 P.M. comes
the Richfield news, after which I go immediately to bed.
I usually twist and turn, worrying about my work until
about midnight. Over the week ends I sleep as long as
I can, wash my hair, occasionally go to a movie by myself

or with a girl friend. Other times I study, mend, or write a letter home about nothing much. I'm quite dull, good-natured, and somewhat easygoing. The girls always know that I never have a date, so I'm the person asked to take telephone and hostess duty in my dormitory and to serve punch at the party. But I'm growing less goodhearted; they frequently have to find some other goat.

Then, too, I'm the person who takes good magazines. I'm the person referred to for topics for themes or term papers, references, or information on such things as the Edict of Nantes. In other words, I seem to be number one Advice Girl.

At parties I'm definitely a flop; therefore, the eats committee is right in my line. Because I'm so busy, I don't have time to get in on one of the games. I always enjoy myself at older people's parties where no fast games, petting, intricate dancing, roughhouse, or risqué stories are involved. I really go so far as to tease and kid older people and enjoy myself very much. But when I try to have a good time with people my own age, I'm as artificial and dull as I can be; I don't understand them. (Don't ever have an only child, even if you have to adopt some more.) To be admitted into my own group, I'll have to force myself to take up games and sports, learn to dance well, get a few muscles and more wind, lose weight, and clear my complexion—everything that I don't care "two hoots" about now. Perhaps I shall be forced to, but not soon.

I'm quite satisfied with the present mold of my life. I have a burning desire for knowledge; to be good, very good, one of the best. I have a goal—to pass the civil service examination for a position in the foreign service. I'm absolutely confident of securing it, because I *will* be one of the best. That aim dictates the major part of my life. Clothes, amusement, play, society, community, hobbies, appearance, activities, and even friends and family, mean hardly a thing. I sometimes wonder if I'm going after it in the right way. I have but a one-track mind; isolation has always been the only way. I must never lose confidence in myself or a certain amount of conceit, because they are the only whips to drive me on. In sustaining them, I sustain myself. When they begin to ebb, I consider suicide—or running away and changing my name. I'm getting a good education; an opportunity awaits me afterward to go on to an absorbing career— the perfect time, the perfect chance for the perfect thing.

Dora's IQ tests show that she is in the upper 20 per cent of her class of 2,000 freshmen. Physically, she is a normal girl—5 feet 6¾ inches tall and weighing 150 pounds. But the significant thing about her is her drive and purpose. She is in the college community, but except for her intellectual interests, one can already see that she is not a part of it. She has no real contact in her social group. In a very definite sense she is not normal in terms of the interests and activities of young people about her. We already know that she is an only child, but that alone could scarcely explain all her drive. She goes on to tell us more about her family, which will throw further light upon her personality and her motivation.

The family includes my father, fifty-eight, blond, tall, very good-natured, witty, uncomplaining, well-liked, and quite a successful and modern farmer. My mother is forty, chubby, short, dark, self-centered, quite likable, a rather poor manager, but better than average house-keeper, not too intelligent, extravagant, in general a very average person, whose constant sniffing and lisping was all right when I was used to it, but now since I've been away, those habits irritate me so much I could scream. She is afraid to go to a doctor to see what is wrong with her nose, even though both Dad and I have wanted her to, ever since I can remember. I try to encourage her to practice some speech exercises that I brought from the speech department, but she is too stubborn, lazy, and annoyingly indifferent to try them.

My father is principally of Danish descent, has lived on the same farm since he was three years old. He went only as far as the eighth grade and is typically prejudiced against Jews, grafters, big business, and everything else conflicting with his interests. He speculated on land dur-ing and after the First World War, and has been paying debts ever since. He is by far one of the hardest workers in the neighborhood as well as one of the largest and most respectable landowners. He belongs to the Grange, a farmers' cooperative, and the Masonic lodge. Dad has modernized his farm machinery and equipment, but not our home, which is owned by his mother. In all, he owns and rents about 2,000 acres. In spite of all his modern equipment, he plants potatoes by the moon and, I am convinced, will continue that practice.

Other than the financial angle, I don't think my father has had a great deal to do with shaping my life. When I was little, he'd tell me stories, but during the depression, he didn't even seem to know that I was around. The few times that he was in the house, he was eating, sleeping, or reading the newspaper. He has tried to get me to become a farmer, since I am expected to be the sole heir to his property. I was given some stock and sent to the Junior Livestock Show for two years, besides being entered in all the girls' divisions. The one principle that my father has developed in me is saving money. I'm going through college so far on my savings and the income from 54 acres of wheat land I'm renting. Dad farms it without pay and gets the sack bills, too. My father is very considerate of all women, but firmly believes I could do anything I trained myself for, if I wanted to.

My mother has greatly encouraged me to study and direct my life in whatever field I should choose. Every week for six years, she went to town to take me for a music lesson. She always bribed or rewarded me (I've never been sure which) for doing good schoolwork, picking up my clothes, sitting straight, doing my chores, and being a good girl. It was usually a pretty dress or money. I was forbidden to do anything which would break my glasses or skin my knee again. . . .

I can remember my mother sending me to school with long underwear, two pairs of woolen stockings, lined boots, my Dad's sheepskin coat, leggings, a quilt, and a special brick heater the first three years of school, so I wouldn't by any possible chance catch cold. That alone would have given anyone an inferiority complex, besides a backache. My desire to be good at studies kept me in during most of the recesses; therefore, my opportunities at play and muscle building were seriously handicapped. My mother, without doubt, has done more to influence me than any other person. She has regulated everything I have done and has seen that I did what was expected. She is somewhat mousy and never says much outside the family. She is the sole person with whom I identify my-self to any large extent. Sometimes I hate that woman enough to choke her, but most all the time I am very grateful to her. One reason for my attitudes is that it seems there is not much difference in our ages—she has never entirely grown up.

One can readily see the roots of some of Dora's interests, ambitions, and motivations in this family situation where the predominating values were work and success through the power of self-directed efforts. In the background is the mother motivating the child by material rewards to meet the standards of excellence she holds for her.

Next to the family, our childhood play group is probably the most deterministic in personality formation. Dora describes her first play group, which had to be outside the family as there were no brothers and sisters, and its effect on her standing in the rural neighborhood.

My first play group I shudder to remember. Before I even started to school, when I was only four years old, three little boys just older than I brought us the mail every day and stayed to play. My sexual experiences began then and lasted till I was nine years old, when my mother decided it was time for me to learn the facts. I was hor-rified at what I'd done, but I didn't tell her. All the kids except me seemed to have been informed long before about such matters, and I had a very bad name. Imme-diately I changed myself completely. I wouldn't even so much as listen to a dirty story. To this day I can count on the fingers of one hand the times I've forced myself to accept a date, but I've never gone twice with the same boy.

The friends I went to school with have never forgotten my soiled record and still remind me of it occasionally, but I weakly try to laugh it off. People always remember the worst things you've done, even though you've completely changed. I don't believe I was ever so happy as the day I heard one boy telling another quite seriously, "I don't care what those fellows got her into, I'm telling you she's the one nice girl there is in this school, and I don't mind telling everybody."

Dora's lack of interest in making heterosexual adjustments and participating in the game of dating and mate seeking, common to young folk of college age, seems not in the least abnormal when one knows of this early experience in her play group and what it cost her in the way of permanent reputation in the only community she knew until she graduated from high school and left for college.

Beyond the play group are the neighborhood and community, ever projecting their values onto the child, offering him experiences or curbing his expressions. What of Dora's neighborhood and community?

The neighborhood is small and "gossipy." Few people have gone further than grade school and most have lived there all their lives. There are few restrictions other than the Ten Commandments. Except for murder and theft, even the Commandments need not be strictly observed. Nice girls are preferred, but the less precise ones are more in demand. One or two families go to church on Easter, but no one thinks of going any other time.

The community centers are widely distributed, three grain warehouses, the school, and a store and post office at a town of about twenty people, including railroad section hands and everybody living 2 or 3 miles out. Most of the marketing and buying is done at a city of over 100,000 population 45 miles distant. Recreational activities are fostered through the school and the Grange. The storekeeper is the postmaster. There is a rural mail route. There is no church; no one wants one.

My home community is quite a contrast to the college life in which I now live. This community is one of youth hailing from every direction and environment for every possible reason. Instead of the quiet, laissez-faire indifference, everyone is in competition with everyone else, particularly in fraternal, dormitory, and clique groups. Older people include mainly the housemothers who maintain order and try to make us all silk-and-satin devotees and oh so, so, precise; who inspect our rooms mainly to see what our personal junk consists of. Their biggest problem is to avoid a complete nervous breakdown. I don't wonder! The professors are not known by the bulk of the student population outside the classroom. Whether they are liked or disliked depends on the number of their witty remarks.

In the home neighborhood Dora has no chance to shed her past. She is known for what she has been as well as for what she is; what she has been affects attitudes of her age group and adults toward her as much as what she is. Both her past and her present determine her reputation in the group.

More significant still is the fact that Dora's past reputation enters into her own conception of herself. Because everybody knows her past, she feels that she is inferior and must always be. Through school she finds an opportunity to compensate for her inferiority feelings by intellectual achievement. With it comes a higher regard for herself.

Thus far, my whole life has been centered around my education. Ever since I started to school, I've been competing. The branches in which I showed success I improved upon; those in which I failed I dropped to a large extent. The home school has an average of 60 students in grade and junior high school and 16 in high school. The main attraction at the beginning of each year is for the students and the neighborhood to see the new teachers. Afterward, the school is one big family settling down to work and basketball games. Everything is quite informal; life is a party, but nobody learns anything worth learning. I have always had a desire to learn at the expense of everything else. I practically memorized my grade-school books; therefore, I did very well. In high school I was forced to play basketball because there were not enough girls to make a team otherwise. I certainly wasn't very much of an asset, and I never did enjoy myself.

I worked in the 4-H club. We had a wonderful leader who required us to enter at the community fair each year which included other clubs. In addition, we gave demonstrations and were taught judging. This club was highly competitive and I was inspired to get blue ribbons, and no matter what the competition was, I got them. Then I tried the livestock division and had the same good fortune. This greatly altered my status in the community.

I was really someone. But the more I did, the more I was expected to do. Besides 4-H regular work, I had to play at the entertainments and give booster talks for the 4-H. I think the 4-H did me more good than any other organization. What it taught me was much less important than the confidence and conceit that it gave me. I knew I could do anything I wanted to and not be afraid.

In my freshman year of high school I changed music teachers from a housewife to the instructor at a teachers' college. I was terribly afraid of this man, but my music progressed by leaps and bounds. My thirteen-year-old eyes had never seen such an immaculate person, never a wrinkle in his clothes that must have been pressed twice a day, never a flaw in speech, well-read, and the cleanest person I've ever seen.

Every night I spent hours washing and ironing clothes and trying to get a flat, sculptured effect on my hair. I bathed three times a day to be sure that I was clean, and I was! I've never put so much time in on myself before nor since, but as soon as I get out of college, I'll do it again. It was worth every minute I spent on myself and hard on the soap and the ironing board. I've forgotten much of the music he taught me, but I certainly shall not forget the lessons in personal care which cost only the time to observe them. This man had been to Europe to study, had collected pictures and autographs of today's well-known musicians. I often wonder if his experiences did not have an unconscious effect upon my final choice of a career in the foreign service. Every cent I ever paid that person was worth ten times the money value.

The music teacher was one of those persons who so often influence the adolescent greatly. In this case, contacts with him gave Dora a conception of a new role for herself. Although she does not say so, she undoubtedly had a "crush" on him and had visions of herself as some day being his wife and accompanying him into the big world beyond her community. There she would be among strangers who knew nothing of her guilty past.

These are the broad outlines of the social processes and group experiences that have formed Dora's personality up to the time she entered college. She writes as a college sophomore unusually industrious scholastically, determined to reach the goal she has set for life, willing to accept her role as a social misfit and be the maternal adviser to girls in her dormitory, and yet recognizing that in many respects she has not arrived at the desired point in her personality development. In her analysis of her present problems there is evidence of conflict and confusion, although there is also evidence that she is defining her life program more and more clearly. Let us consider further some of her adjustment difficulties. First, she relates certain of her problems to her own biological development and to the social responses her physical characteristics have elicited from associates.

> I resemble both my parents in various ways. From my mother came defective eyesight, a tendency toward obesity, dark eyes. From my Dad, height, color of hair, and some facial features. The worst worries I have are my acne skin and dreadful rheumatism appearing at the most unexpected places. About all one can do for both is to grow out of them, if possible. . . .
>
> I've always been much older appearing than the people my age. Because I was grown up when I was ten,

everyone always expected a great deal of me. Naturally one has to live up to social expectations at the expense of really getting the worth out of childhood. People used to ask me if I were in high school when I was in the sixth grade. Now they think I'm a graduate student in college. Even my own associates accept me as someone older than they, but the older people accept me as someone younger. I can't see that I fit into any group; so I have to fit myself much of the time. I have been too old for a kid and too young for a woman. I am beginning to fear that the situation will always remain thus.

In addition to the social reactions to her biological make-up, which give her a sense of isolation and aloneness, Dora feels sensitive about her inability to participate in the social world.

I am often ashamed of my inability and ignorance in the social world, but I try to laugh it off by saying that I can't do everything. I'm going to try to direct my summers to achieving more social ease. . . .

My inferiority in a recreational sense has mainly been overcome by compensating through studying. I am beginning to wonder if this is the right way after all. I could overcome it if I took time. In being successful in the foreign service, the more accomplishments one has, the better chance of success. Next summer I have resolved to learn some sports, dancing, improve my French, learn to play a horn, and become much better informed on all subjects. I think I need to see the other side of life, but I don't have time at college. . . .

In everything that I do well I have a superiority com-

plex. I don't doubt at all that I carry it to the extreme.
Just the other day a fellow said, "That girl is certainly
stuck up." I can see that I'm going to need some polishing
on myself to give just the right effect, but I'm going to
have to change the composition, too. I can't do it over-
night, though. . . .

Yet people say, "Dora, I'd give anything to play and sing
like you," or "How in the world do you make your
grades?" or "What pretty teeth you have, Grandmother."
For a time I think I'm not such a washout after all. Maybe
people really do like me and I'm making mountains. If
I would take the time for silly and confidential matters,
I could have a great many friends. But if I had a lot of
friends, they would bother me so much that I couldn't
work. It seems to be an endless chain, and where the weak
link is I don't know. May I repeat: I can't do everything.
I have neither the capacity nor the ability to manage
it. . . .

Dora's conception of herself is by no means clear. Most
of the time she feels quite certain that she is inferior socially. At other times, when a bit of praise or flattery comes
her way, she feels socially adequate. Maybe she is accepted
after all; maybe at least as fully as she wishes to be. So the
quandary goes and probably will until she either acquires
social ease among her own age group or becomes so firmly
established in her vocation that continuous ego support
will be derived from a successful and unchallenged role
there.

In the meantime, the going is sometimes difficult. She
resorts to daydreaming. From what we know of her already, it is easy to imagine the content of these dreams.

I regret that I am very subject to daydreaming. I picture myself in foreign lands learning their customs and having a very difficult but most enjoyable excursion. . . .

The problem that has faced me ever since I graduated from the eighth grade is that of an occupation. I thought and thought and thought and thought—nursing, medicine, law, farming, teaching, music? I had always expected to go to college, but even when I came, I took a general course for want of something definite. Then I thought of speech. In music I did very well in my voice lessons under a teacher who spent much extra time to encourage me. Last summer I reached the point where I didn't care what I was. I took a trip off to Montana, went swimming, learned to ride horseback, and quit worrying. Then one day something just said to me, "Why don't you try history? You never stopped liking it and you do very well in it. You have a desire to learn what the world is about. You're broad-minded enough to see that it doesn't consist of just what you know. You're ignorant of everything but what you've contacted. You're not afraid of work. Try the foreign service; see the world and what makes it turn. Improve yourself by associating with the people who are doing these things—the men who have gone somewhere and are guiding the whole world. Have enough ability and you can pass any civil service exam." That's my goal and all the talent, ability, and ambition I can gather won't be one unit too much to take me on from here.

Although fantasy has played a great part in Dora's thinking, she comes back from the dream world to face the realistic problems her decision implies and drives forward

fully conscious of obstacles in the way of making her
dreams a reality.

My whole life will no doubt be a struggle to achieve
equal ability with men in a man's position. The head of
my department has frankly told me that I shall have to
be twice as good as the average man to even break into
the foreign service. I can be and I will; it means that
much to me. I know that I myself and all my benefactors
will realize that all the added effort is entirely worth
while.

I feel that the main reason women are not treated
equally in business is because they are inferior, both in
experience and knowledge. My goal is to never stop learning. During the winter I open the doors intellectually;
from now on, in the summer, I'll open the doors socially
as much as possible. I realize that I shall have to do that
and can only with great difficulty.

At present, except for relatives, I'm inclined to accept
all men on an impersonal basis. I always judge them by
their intelligence and ambition rather than by appearance
alone. The best-looking men are usually low in the other
respects. They know they can get by on their looks. I feel
that marriage would ruin everything for me; so I dis-
courage friendliness with men as politely as I can. I think
the greatest trouble I shall have in a man's world is my
being reared in a woman's world. I can see that I'm breaking away from women's standards more and more every
day. Perhaps I shall have that adjustment well begun
before I have to face it.

Clearly the one thing that holds Dora together, the
motive force, is her desire to achieve her goal of competi-

tive success in passing a civil service examination to enter the foreign service. She is centering all her energies on this goal.

As we review Dora's present personality, it is clear that the motivations that seemed rather peculiar at the outset for a girl of seventeen are in reality not so when one understands the social processes that have formed her during the years from childhood to adulthood; in fact, it seems quite natural that she would be the kind of person she is. Certainly teachers who worked with her in high school needed to know a great deal more about Dora Dover than that she had a high intelligence-test score. Intelligence is not the key to her personality. To understand Dora, one must know that she has one overpowering ambition compared with which life itself means nothing.

Behind it is no doubt a desire to shed her past, escape into the big anonymous world of foreign travel, and work with strangers.

You and I are in a position to see through Dora's motives and drives and to appraise them. She probably was not. Was she going places or only running away from guilt, which was carried over from the innocent indiscretions of childhood, her failure to accept herself, and her failure to accept the normal female role?

Is there much likelihood of her realizing her goal or fitting the role she dreams of if she should attain this goal?

I have not been able to follow Dora's career and do not know whether she completed college, and if she did, what occupation she entered. I can only guess, as you can, how she came out.

Knowing that she was confused, should she not have taken time out to have worked with a counselor, taken tests to appraise her ability and aptitudes, and tried by such devices to get a true appraisal of herself and her motivations?

And had she talked with some mature and understanding counselor about her childhood sex experience, which was so much a part of her difficulty now, would she have gone on trying to cover up and have continued to feel guilty?

Dora had more problems than she could handle alone, but at the time she wrote her autobiography, she was driving herself ahead at full speed. But was she accomplishing anything or merely escaping from herself? If the latter is true, the time would surely come when she would have to be brought face to face with her limitations and when she would have to reappraise all her plans and purposes.

CHAPTER XIII

The Destiny within Me

Problems of religion and secularism

Ernie Pyle, who wrote more intimately of life on the battle front than any other journalist, and who lost his life while in the front lines, talked about soldiers needing a stake in the future in order to have a motive for fighting and enduring hardship.

We all need a stake in the future, a faith that will make us strive to use the resources that are within us to achieve a destiny.

Bob Richards, the preacher athlete who has almost tied the world record for the pole vault, and who expects to break it yet, always prays before making an attempt to go over the pole. The cynics say he is praying to win; the mockers that he is trying to vault his way to heaven. Richards says this of his prayers:

> Sure, I pray. But it's not for divine help to achieve such a silly, temporal thing as winning an athletic event. I try to go deep within myself to find the power and inherent strength I need. No man has a right to ask God's help unless he is willing to extend himself. Jesus said all things are possible if you'll only believe. Faith in Him will move

mountains. It is that faith I try to marshal when I pray in
sports. . . .

Faith to rally our resources and use them to achieve our
goals is the difference in most lives between being all we
are capable of and being less than we might be.

We may not be religious, but we cannot live without
faith. If we have religion, we have faith—faith in a power
beyond ourselves. Often religion is an important influence
in strengthening faith in ourselves.

The atmosphere of the large college campus today is
quite secular. Religion as such frequently has little place,
and at many points secular teachings of science may conflict with our conservative religious knowledge. This often
puts faith to a severe test. It is not uncommon for the college young person to experience some bewilderment as
the old foundations of faith are shaken and he casts about
for new ones.

"Now I am at college, an English major, a sorority
pledge," Eve writes. "I still think it is a waste of time and
money to be here. College has managed to take away to
some degree my self-confidence, faith in humanity, and
religion. College has given me restlessness, dissatisfaction,
distrust of nearly all people, and a surface hardness or
cynicism."

Luanne has begun to question and doubt, as all young
people do at some period in their teens.

> All of my life I have wrestled with religious conflicts.
> While still a child, I wondered if God would ever forgive
> me if I did not become a foreign missionary. In my home

religion was a basic factor of consideration. It was taken for granted that church attendance be regular. I never questioned the lessons taught, the stories told, or the theories advanced. My mother is a firm, though unde-monstrative, believer in religion. My father has never expressed his belief in any manner; yet, whether it is religion or not, he has a definite set of ethics, a well-defined code of right and wrong that closely governs his actions. Perhaps I am like my father, with definite rules but no expressed opinion of religion. The recreational social groups, particularly my friends, have generally had a religious basis of activity. A mild type of dual person-alities has thus developed. At college my actions of ethics are based on the rules alone; in my home village, I ac-cept the beliefs of my friends in their various groups of truly religious life. There has never been a definite settlement in my mind of what constitutes religion and of what one's beliefs should consist.

My childhood faith was broken by my first contact with evolutionary theories. The impression of ancestral apes was so strongly pictured that it served as the first severing factor. Gradually intellectual advances widened the breach until now I have a definite conflict to deal with, both at home and at college. Dangerous questions some-times arise in periods of despondency—just what is our purpose in life? and why are we living?

Morgan has reached at least a tentative conclusion.

One conflict which arises in the lives of nearly all stu-dents is confronting me. It is a conflict of original religious training versus science. In my case it has not caused the

difficulty which many experience. I have quietly ration-
alized on the subject and decided in favor of a scientific
explanation to all phenomena. This is due probably to
my open-mindedness and to the fact that early religious
training was not embedded with a great deal of fervor.
Although my convictions on religion have undergone
great alteration, I am aiming to retain a basis for proper
conduct which is, I believe, dictated by society.

Bart has decided to let things work themselves out.

I realize I will have to change my stolid views on
several matters pertaining to religion. I just cannot believe some of the things set forth to us in the Sunday school
and church. Do not think that I do not believe in religion,
for I do. I think it is a potent influence in most people's
lives, but I do convincingly believe that I will have to
be more tolerant. Science has proved that some of the
things set forth in Christianity cannot be absolutely true.
The Bible was written by human beings, and therefore
cannot be perfect. These things have caused quite a conflict in my mind, but I am going to try to forget about
them and let them take their own course.

*What research shows regarding young people's
religious concerns*

Psychologists Kuhlen and Arnold, in a study of 547
young people, examined the shift in concern over various
religious problems from age twelve to eighteen. Here are
the proportion of young people of various ages checking
the problems listed:

Religious Problems of the Teen Years (Problems checked as sometimes or often present) *

PROBLEM	AGE OF YOUNG PERSONS		
	12 years	15 years	18 years
Having a different religion from other people	34	25	27
Disliking church service	33	47	60
Being forced to go to church	30	31	27
Disliking parents' religion	11	8	12
Failing to go to church	67	67	67
Changing my idea of God	29	25	31
Losing faith in religion	27	32	31
Doubting prayer will bring good	37	44	35
Getting help on religious problems	53	54	56
Choosing a religion	21	20	15
Parents' objection to church membership	23	14	11
Wanting to know the meaning of religion	53	48	60
Wanting communion with God	59	47	57
Heaven and hell	53	53	66
Sin	71	62	72
Conflicts of science and religion	42	50	57
Being teased about my religious feelings	26	22	18
Wondering what becomes of people when they die	67	56	80
Number of cases	174	243	130

* Raymond G. Kuhlen and Martha Arnold, "Age Differences in Religious Beliefs and Problems during Adolescence," *Pedagogical Seminar and Journal of Genetic Psychology*, 65:296, December, 1944.

The old problem of denominational differences

Denominations are a part of American religious life. The U.S. Census listed 212 different denominations in its last survey of religious bodies. Even then it often combined smaller religious bodies. An earlier census listed 236.

Denominations all build their religious beliefs about various Christian principles, but they differ greatly in the kind of behavior they expect of their followers. This often becomes a source of confusion as young people of different church backgrounds associate. Here is one example of how it works:

> The first difficult decision I was forced to make had to do with the conflict of religious ideals. I had always taken the same attitudes toward religion as my mother and father, who had more than likely received their interpretation of religion from their parents. They believed that shows, dances, and cards were perfectly all right as long as they didn't interfere with going to church every Sunday. When I became a junior in high school, I became friendly with several girls who had been brought up to believe that it was sinful and evil to do these things. I was in their company a great deal and became influenced by their religious beliefs. The conflict of the two produced a certain degree of confusion. It puzzled me a great deal as to which of these two beliefs was right and which I should accept. After debating with myself a great deal, and reasoning it out, I finally came to the decision that there was nothing wrong with dances, shows, and cardplaying if they didn't interfere with the morals my folks had followed through their lives, and as long as I associated with the right company.

Sue faces these differences in religion in her college associations.

> I am not conscious of any religious prejudice. One of my Jewish classmates gives me unleavened bread at Christmas time, and some of my closest friends are Catho-

lics. However, there has been a strong inhibition developed against allowing friendship with Catholic boys to grow into intimacy. This has been quite a serious conflict for me. I realize that young couples are much happier when they have a common religion, but I rationalize and wonder if they cannot develop a "halfway" mark. This will probably be one of the serious problems I will have to face in the next year or two.

Shall I marry across religious lines?

Sue, in her dating, already is thinking about the problems of a mixed-religion marriage. If she should continue dating with those of different religion, she will eventually have to face the question.

What is the answer?

As with so many decisions in life, there is no one answer. There is, however, some research on the problem which is at least a partial guide, in that the experiences of many are likely to be better than our own individual experience or ideas on the problem.

The chart shows the results of a study of over 4,000 marriages. Religious difference is a hazard.

It is interesting to note, however, that marriage across religious lines, except in the case of a Catholic father and Protestant mother, is not so great a risk as marriage between those with no religion at all. Other studies of marriage happiness, too, show that religious training is favorably related to successful adjustment in marriage.

What about marriage across denominational lines? There is actually little difference in beliefs and practices of most Protestant denominations. Unless one is overly serious about the specific practices and teachings of his denomination, there is likely to be no problem, particularly for college graduates, who should acquire some tolerance toward minor religious differences.

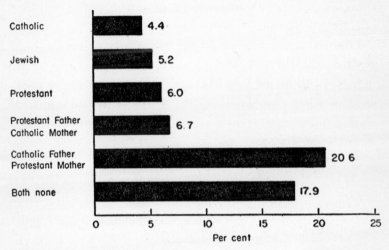

Proportion of homes broken by divorce or separation by religious affiliation (based on a study of 4,108 marriages). (Based on data from Judson T. Landis, "Marriages of Mixed and Non-mixed Religious Faiths," American Sociological Review, *14:403, June, 1949.)*

There may be some difficulties if one comes from a sectarian group with revivalistic procedures and the other from a church that is formal and ritualistic. The differences may be on aesthetic and appreciation levels rather than on belief as such.

The broadening process

We need not fear the natural broadening of our religious or moral beliefs as we approach maturity. College experience may force this broadening a little more rapidly than it would have come otherwise, but most of us experience it eventually.

Often the standards of our own family or other small groups have been unduly severe, and we must change somewhat to fit the larger society. Here a young man tells of his mother's rigid codes from which he is seeking to escape. The fact that he can see them clearly enough to write about them indicates that he is on his way.

> The philosophy of my mother is uniquely her own. Its definition of social strata is its own. It recognizes the highest stratum as those who are "good"—not necessarily clever, powerful, intelligent, wealthy, but "good." This, of course, carries its own concept of good. There are more negatives than positives to this concept. Having had her share of drunkards in her own family, liquor is the great evil and to drink destroys all good in a person. If a person is too vivacious, that person becomes overbearing and is no longer good. Smoking undermines the health, and consequently lowers the social stature of whoever dares to do so. A person must fulfill all of his potentialities in all fields or is open to censure. A person who is not attentive or observant and fails to tip his hat or nod and speak is liable to find that he has become snobbish and is no longer good. Nice people don't read any of the recent novels of the type dealing with oversexed females and the

existence of a known wanton is not recognized by good people—she is considered dead and in hell.

It is difficult to express this entire philosophy on paper, but it is common enough that these examples should suffice. It is strongly individualistic and unswerving, and judges all else accordingly, avoiding that which disagrees and slowly withdrawing into its own shell.

A college girl tells of broadening her moral code to the point of tolerance for behavior which in her former group was always condemned. "In high school," she writes, "my ideas and attitudes were usually the same as my parents'. In college I have had to make decisions of my own without any outside help. Also many of my attitudes have changed. From my studies I have learned to be tolerant of the other fellows' actions and habits. For instance, in my home town I always looked upon a man that drank as unintelligent and of a low status in society, but here at college where I see even college instructors drinking, I cannot help but conclude that I have had a narrow view. Consequently, I am learning a somewhat more tolerant attitude toward them."

In our younger days our thinking was limited to the beliefs and traditions of our local church and childhood group. Adulthood, wherever achieved, consists of considering the views of others, experiencing a conflict of belief systems, and working out a more rational basis for our own beliefs.

The anxieties and fears that young people so often experience during their early college days, while very real, must be recognized as a process of growing up. It will help us if we can puzzle less over our conflicts of belief and keep before us the clear goal of serving and preparing to serve others, of being useful and planning greater usefulness. This will help ease our worries and at the same time lead us toward our goals. In time it will clarify our thinking about our destiny.

CHAPTER XIV

Getting Started in Studies

Experience itself is perhaps the best teacher. We learn quicker by trying to do something than by merely being told how. This fact is especially true of learning the best way to study and prepare for college classes. After a few weeks of going to Dr. Blank's classes, you will discover just what kind of notes he wants, what kind of papers he expects, and what kind of exams he gives. But there are a few study techniques that are always desirable, regardless of what class or even what school you are in. Any student will have an easier time, especially in the confusion and uncertainty of the first few weeks, if he has these techniques well in mind from the outset.

High school was never like this

One of the first things a freshman discovers is the great difference between studying for high-school classes and those of college. In the first place, high-school teachers seem very concerned about how their students get along, whether or not they understand the work, and whether they are keeping up with the assignments. They give special help when it is needed and often give class time to prepare for assignments. Many students experience a catastrophe, such as Henry recounts here, before they get wise to the unfamiliar and impersonal business of preparing for college classes. He wrote:

> At the first class meeting, our Psych I instructor casually announced that we were to have read the first ten chapters of the textbook by Friday of the fourth week of school. He said that, unless we asked questions, he would assume that we were having no difficulty with reading and understanding it. That was the only announcement he made. For the next few weeks, he lectured on various things and said nothing more about assignments. I decided psych was a snap.
>
> Then one day after about a month of school we found an examination waiting for us when we entered the classroom. I'll never forget the howls of agony that went up. At least half of the class, including yours truly, had never cracked the book.

The student is more on his own in doing college work than he ever was in high school. Many professors don't even bother to call the roll. As one chem prof put it, "I don't care where they learn the material—in class or at a soda fountain—just so they know it by exam time." Many students have a difficult time adjusting to this new independence and self-direction. For some, the soda fountain or the student lounge is just too great a temptation. "I'll work twice as hard tomorrow and make up for it," they tell themselves. But students who can cut classes and still do good work are few and far between.

This does not mean that college teachers are completely

indifferent to whether we sink or swim. As a matter of fact, most of them are willing to give some individual help if we ask for it. But the difference between the high-school and college teacher is this: The high-school teacher sought out the troubled and confused students, practically forcing them to accept help, the college teacher assumes that his students are old enough and wise enough to know when they need help and to ask him or someone else for help if they need it.

Managing our time

Most freshmen experience a rude awakening along about the second week or so of school. At first, the idea of having each class only every other day, often only once or twice a week, seems wonderful. From the end of the class on Monday morning until it meets again on Wednesday seems like a small eternity. But they soon learn that the fewer the class meetings, the larger the assignments. Then, too, colleges texts aren't written as simply as high-school books. As one student put it, "I never sit down with just my text, but always with two books. One is inevitably Webster's dictionary." Another student admitted, "I always read my assignments at least twice. The first reading gives me an idea of what the author is talking about. The second time around I begin to understand what he is talking about—(sometimes)."

So the belief that there is plenty of time for everything soon evaporates. By the second month or so most freshmen are wondering how in the world they can ever finish all their assignments in the time allowed.

Managing time demands a schedule—not just a "more-or-less" schedule in our minds, but one that is carefully thought out, detailed, and right there in black and white so we can't ignore it. A schedule should allot time for each of the major activities throughout the day—classes, meals, special recreation, sleep, and study.

Some students deplore the idea of scheduling their time, feeling that it takes all the freedom and joy out of life. But here is the other side of the argument, as suggested by a college senior:

> I used to think schedules were for bookworms and other kinds of lowly life, but along about my sophomore year I became so involved in activities along with my studies that I finally decided to try a schedule. I discovered that I actually had more free time and more time for purely social interests than before. With a schedule, I knew just what had to be done and exactly when and where I should do it. This way I got things out of the way instead of worrying and putting them off.

When it comes to scheduling time for class preparation, it is *not* enough merely to indicate certain hours for study. The schedule should tell us exactly what to study during each half hour or so of our study time. Here is the Tuesday-morning schedule of a sophomore honor student:

7:00   Breakfast and room duty
8:00   Chem. 1 lecture in Room 407, Science Building
9:00   Review notes from chem lecture in library
9:30   Review assignment for Soc. 11 in library
10:00   Soc. 11 lecture in Room 7, McKinnley Hall
11:00   Quickly review notes from Soc. 11 lecture in library

11:30   Read Chem. 1 assignment for Thursday
12:00   Lunch

Here is the same student's Tuesday-evening schedule:

5:00   Dinner
6:00   Dorm meeting
6:30   Meet Bill at Union Building lounge
7:15   Review soc. text notes and lecture notes for last week
7:30   Read soc. assignment due Thursday morning
8:00   Type English theme due each Friday
8:45   Ten-minute break for a coke
9:00   Quickly review psych lecture notes
9:15   Read psych assignment due Thursday afternoon
10:00   Ten-minute break for stretch and fresh air
10:15   Review class notes and assignment for English 11 due
        Wednesday morning
10:30   Bath, etc.
11:00   Bed

In looking over this schedule, notice that on Tuesday evening this student did not just prepare for the next day's classes but for a number of different things. She refreshed her memory on what she had learned that day by going over the class notes she had taken. She scheduled the typing of a weekly theme three days before it was due and thus saved herself from last-minute rush and worry. She allowed more time for reading her psych than for reading her soc. assignment, probably because the former was more difficult for her. She scheduled a review of the assignment due in her Wednesday morning's English class so that she would be fresh on the subject and able to contribute to class discussion. She arranged two 10-minute breaks in the course of her 3-hour study period because she had discovered that after such breaks she could work faster and better than by plugging along with a tired, tense mind.

This student generally followed this Tuesday-evening schedule religiously week after week. She did not, however, feel enslaved to the schedule. When an especially good movie was showing at a local theater, she did not feel that she was bound to miss it. Neither did she toss her schedule out when such "exceptional" things arose. She took time out to *reschedule* her time for the evening. Perhaps she skipped her regular Tuesday-evening after-dinner date with Bill and did some work before going to the theater. Some of her Tuesday-evening work was done earlier in the day; a little of it was left over for some free time on Wednesday. Before thinking about a movie, however, she always made sure that she would have sufficient time to make up for the work she missed on the evening out. Taking these precautions added to the fun of her evening off because she felt no guilt or worry over having neglected her assignments.

A good schedule is never a ball and chain. One of its values is its flexibility. By leaving an occasional hour or so completely undesignated for any task, we leave ourselves room for special or unexpected events. Such free time allows for the occasional shifting of study so that we need not miss out on unscheduled experiences.

Taking notes

Note taking is a completely new experience for most college students. Very few high-school teachers use the lecture system that is so common in college. Freshmen are likely to be overwhelmed at the prospect of having to listen, understand, retain, and take notes all at the same time. Many of them pay little attention to the meaning of the lecture and never stop to ask themselves if they really understand what it's all about. This is a result of over-emphasizing the importance of notes. Some even wish they knew shorthand so they wouldn't miss a word of the prof's lecture.

As a matter of fact, most students take far too many notes. Lectures are meant to be listened to and understood. Notes are valuable as reminders of important points the prof has made. They certainly need not be verbatim records of his every word.

A good plan to follow in note taking involves three steps:

1. Listen to what the professor says.
2. Say it over to yourself in your own words to see if you really understand it.
3. Write down in abbreviated form the gist of his main ideas, using only cue words and phrases, not complete sentences.

Always go over your class notes as soon after class as possible (no later than the evening of the same day). While they are still fresh in mind, you can fill out important ideas that you may have noted too briefly. At this time you should clearly differentiate main topics from subtopics by underlining, Roman numerals, or some other device. Some students can outline easily as they take notes. Most of us are not quite so thorough, and if we stop to organize as we go along, it is easy to get so involved that we miss important points.

This early review of our notes has an additional value. Our memories are such that we forget things fastest in the first few hours after we have learned them. This review refreshes our minds on the new points and greatly reduces the amount of forgetting that would normally take place.

Think as *you read*

I once interrupted a young friend who was poring over his textbook and asked him to tell me briefly just what he was reading. His answer was about what I expected. "I don't know what I'm reading," he admitted. "I haven't yet stopped to think it over." Many students mistakenly believe that they save time by reading an assignment at breakneck speed and then stopping to figure out what it said. Most textbooks are written to be studied, not just skimmed. By the time he gets around to "thinking it over," the average student has forgotten many of the author's most important points. Some must even waste the time they have just saved by reading the very same material a second time.

Reading an assignment thoughtfully may take a little longer, but it saves time in the long run. By carefully noting the chapter heading and subtitles, we have a clear idea concerning what we are going to read in a chapter, and by mentally going over what we have just read, we get a clearer picture of the topic as a whole and the significance of each subtopic. Some experts even advise turning each subtitle within a chapter into a question and then trying to answer the question after the unit has been read.

The important thing, however, is to read and think at the same time. Whenever you discover your mind slipping off into daydreams as you absently skim the words, pull back to reality. After a week or so of enforced concentration, you will find that you get more from your assignments with just one reading when the reading is accompanied by thought.

Review frequently; don't cram

It isn't enough just to keep up with our assignments from day to day. Our instructors expect us not only to learn the subject matter but also to remember it. Regardless of how carefully you study a certain assignment in November, chances are you will forget most of it by January (semester-exam time) *unless* you schedule frequent reviews during the two-month period.

A Phi Beta Kappa from a Southern university attributed his good grades primarily to frequent reviews. He wrote:

> When I was a freshman I was all eyes and ears on the subject of "how to study." I'd carefully watch the older fellows in the house to see how they studied. What I saw was a shock. Most of them sloughed off on daily reading and by exam time they had forgotten nine-tenths of what they had read. Nearly every one of them burned the midnight oil cramming just before the final exam. I wondered how I could manage to do college work well if I followed their example. I hit upon the idea of reviews and soon began briefly reviewing each subject for about fifteen

minutes every week. At each review I'd read slowly and carefully through my class notes and then I'd look through the text, noting the important points that I had underlined as I read it the first time.

Review is not merely a matter of reading over notes and parts of the textbook that have been underscored. Even more important to memory is what the psychologist calls "recall." We must practice recalling what we have gone over. The most effective method of fixing subject matter in mind is to sit down and recall as much of it as possible. After this, notes should be checked to fix attention on the things which have been forgotten. Each review should begin by recalling all that can be remembered and reviewing what has not been recalled. By this method, each succeeding review leaves less to be studied.

These are but a few of the many study techniques a good student will learn during his first year or so in college. But it is surprising how many students continue to barely get by merely for lack of better study habits. The difference between an A and a C student is often not in how much time they study but in how well they use the time that they do spend. A carefully prepared time schedule coupled with better note taking, thoughtful textbook reading, frequent reviews, and deliberate practice at recall are some of the basic aspects of really sound study habits. Knowing them in advance can make your first weeks of college less worrisome.

CHAPTER XV

What Should College Expect of Me?

College is organized on the assumption that young people who attend it are sufficiently mature to manage their own affairs as adults. There are more protections and disciplines than in the work world of adults outside, but many fewer than most young people have experienced before. How to learn to use freedom and opportunity is the real test of adulthood.

There are requirements

Those who finish a college curriculum successfully are granted a degree. This degree will mean that the graduate represents the college and its training program for the rest of his life. If college degrees are to mean anything, and if a particular college is to maintain a reputation for doing its work well, certain requirements have to be met.

Requirements are never fully satisfactory. They mean that we must take some courses and have classes with some professors of little or no interest. This is part of the price of obtaining a degree. Electives are more pleasant, but often the requirements, which seemed so foolish, unnecessary, or difficult, also prove to be worth while.

173

There have, of course, been geniuses who refused to harness themselves with college requirements and quit rather than face the music. Great authors, inventors, and other persons of distinction have sometimes been in the group who decided to go out on their own rather than face up to irksome requirements.

We shall, however, find more, even of the geniuses, who saw it through and profited by the experience.

Life everywhere is full of requirements. It is a part of adulthood to meet them.

Social life

For many there is too much social life on the college campus; for some, too little. A balanced social life is desirable for the well-rounded personality. While some scientists or authors may live introvertedly, most human beings need, as well as enjoy, the social side of life.

College should help correct aspects of personality that have been a little out of balance, that is, for those who are willing to look themselves over and work at it. Those who are inclined to be too bookwormish should throw the books aside on Friday or Saturday night for some social life. Those who have done little else but socialize should begin to act like adults and settle down to a fixed routine of work, putting it ahead of bull sessions and dances.

Sleep

I suppose there is no group alive that sleeps so little at night and dozes so much during the day at their work and in classes as do college students. There is so much going

on around the college campus that many think they can't
miss any of it. There is no time to sleep. In dull lethargy
they ponder over textbooks during the wee hours and take
pills to keep awake all night before exams. Such behavior
indicates poor management of time.

A few can get along for quite a period on four or five
hours of sleep. But no one can enjoy life that way.

Some break in health or nerves under the strain, and
others who succeed in carrying on through college with
little sleep may take six months or more to rest up afterward.

College isn't the real marathon. That begins in the
adult world in parenthood and business or professional
competition. It is well to conserve a little steam for the
long pull ahead.

It is a part of maturity to be able to leave some things
out of the program. At no time in life will anyone be able
to participate in everything or be a part of all that goes on.
Selective participation in things which lead in the direction one wishes to go is the secret of achieving success, as
well as of having time.

Concentration on the task at hand

As important as having a regular study schedule, such
as the one shown in Chapter XIV, is the cultivation of the
habit of pitching in and working when one is at it. This
means getting at hand everything one needs to work with.
It means getting at the job promptly, without a lot of
wishing and groaning and daydreaming. It means concentration on the task at hand rather than dreaming about

last week's date or the one coming tomorrow. This capacity to concentrate will grow with practice.

Many who go to college expect to be leaders in the professions when their degrees are granted. The professions mean a lifetime of study and concentration. If one is in college simply for the prestige the degree adds to social or business life, he can perhaps afford to drift along. But if he has goals which will require the use of his creative gifts, he must cultivate the mind and develop its powers or be a cripple in his future work.

Steps toward moral maturity may well begin with facing the music in class performance. It is part of adulthood to take the responsibility for the outcome of one's own performance. In any case, when examinations come around, as they do so regularly, it doesn't do much good to say, "That mean prof gave me an F!" The prof will not admit that he gave you anything. He will say, "Every student in my classes gets exactly what he earns." Usually his examination is objective, and often scored by a machine, so students cannot argue very convincingly about where their scores fall in the normal curve.

On the matter of basic honesty, college is the last proving ground before complete adulthood. Many schools have an honor system. Some do not; but in either case life has one, and those who cheat not only dishonor themselves and their group but prove themselves unworthy of college opportunity.

Moral maturity does not always come easy, and there is too little of it in all circles, but it is the price of many opportunities and satisfactions throughout life.

One reason it is so often difficult to measure up is that our culture sets so high a value on the goal of winning that there is always a temptation to take short cuts.

Basketball scandals in major universities indicate how easy it is to step from the athletic scholarship to accepting a bribe. The dropping of a long list of men from West Point in 1952 for violating the honor system against cheating in examinations is illustrative of the temptation to succeed at the cost of honor. Some thought the penalty was too severe, but do we want men in positions of military leadership who cannot abide by an honor code in college? Would these men perhaps also violate the code of honesty later in handling great sums of money, directing the interest and welfare of subjected peoples, or managing large groups of military personnel and property put under their charge? Certainly cheating in examinations does not always carry over to cheating in life, but it often does. Why take the chance, when honorable men are available?

I personally have always scrupulously followed the practice of never recommending those whom I know to be dishonest in college matters, and will not permit a candidate to work with me toward an advanced degree if he has proved himself to be dishonest. I know that many, perhaps most of my colleagues, hold the same standard.

Stakes in the future

This brings us to the problem of planting stakes in the future—goals to work toward, ends to be achieved. The person who knows where he is going has several advantages. He can take the nearest and best route to his destination. The one who doesn't is a hobo who, having no destination, doesn't know whether he is headed toward it and wouldn't know if he got there.

We need destinations in the three fields mentioned before: (1) the moral field, (2) the economic field, and (3) the marital field. Society expects all persons, but particularly those who are gifted, to achieve adulthood in all these fields. College is the time not only to move rapidly toward these goals but actually to achieve them.

The first two goals have been discussed at some length already, so we shall only summarize these goals and dwell mostly on attaining marital maturity.

Realizing the goal of moral maturity

The college-trained should be leaders in moral behavior as well as in scholarship. They have had the advantage of acquiring the American traditions of freedom, integrity, democracy, tolerance, and honesty. They should demand of themselves goodness and integrity.

"Can the blind lead the blind? Shall they not both fall into the ditch?" A society which grants the privilege of much training to a select group of its members has a right to expect a high level of moral integrity of them, for they are to be its leaders.

Realizing economic maturity

For most young people, as we have suggested earlier, college has an economic motivation along with whatever particular values they seek to achieve. At the end of the college curriculum is the job. Just what job is not always known at the beginning, but all young people hope that the job will be waiting, for they can scarcely extend their period of preparaton for life much beyond college. A few who go on to graduate or professional school can, although most of them earn their way by obtaining teaching or research fellowships; others have to enter immediately into the world of work.

The development of work habits, a sense of responsibility to discharge obligations, an ability to persist until the goal is reached—virtues which we have stressed repeatedly—are all a vital part of preparation for economic maturity. Work is the most persistent, time-consuming activity of adult waking life. The sooner we become reconciled to this fact, the better we are able to face it.

Finding the right work is one of the big objectives of the college experience. Most work requires only general training, but to be in the job or occupation for which one is fitted by temperament and interest is for a lifetime of happiness, the next most important thing to making the right kind of marriage.

No one should be embarrassed at taking all the tests available to learn his aptitudes. College is the time to make sure one is headed in the right direction occupationally.

Realizing marital maturity

Joke as we may about it, colleges and universities are marriage factories. They should be. One of the fine things about this is that the marriages of college students in general turn out much better than those of the population at large.

This is partly, no doubt, because college students marry a little later in life and have the advantages of more mature judgment in selecting a mate. It is due in part to the fact that most college campuses offer courses in marriage and parenthood which help students to prepare for it. Some campuses have marriage counseling services where pre-marital advice may be obtained.

Dating is fun, and a certain amount of shopping around is desirable, but the time comes when society expects all to marry and take on the responsibilities of dependents.

For the college girl particularly, the time is short. Once she graduates and enters the usual women's professional occupations—nursing, library work, and teaching—she has little contact with marriageable men. Her chances of marriage drop rapidly after she graduates. The picto-

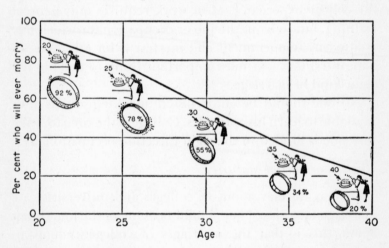

Chances of marriage for women decline rapidly with increasing years. By age thirty, they are little more than fifty-fifty.

graphic chart shows how the chances drop for all women as their ages increase. They drop even faster for college women.

Men in our society still prefer to marry women who will worship their husband's accomplishments rather than overshadow them. This is Dr. Paul Popenoe's opinion, based on counseling work in the American Institute of Family Relations in Los Angeles. Men are not interested in a woman's college degree, but in her warmth, understanding, affection, and tenderness. Dr. Popenoe warns the college woman that she must not neglect the cultivation of these qualities in her personality during the college career.

Some experts feel that the rigid discipline of scholarship—putting off present pleasure for future gain—may dull these qualities in women. Their opinion is supported by the situation that Deborah describes. She writes:

> I have enjoyed college tremendously ever since I arrived. I can literally feel myself changing, and I honestly believe the changes are all for the better. I'm neater and much more considerate since I share a dorm room, rather than having a room of my own. I've got a quicker, clearer mind and much more self-assurance since I've been subjected to the brisk discussions of many of my classes.
>
> Still, in the back of my mind there is a growing uncertainty as to what all this will mean in my future. Even today, after only a few months of college, I know that I would be less acceptable to most fellows as a wife than when I first came. I'm too opionionated, too independent and ambitious. I have the terrible feeling that after four years I could never play the part of the self-effacing, hero-worshipping wife that most men want.

This case gets at the root of the problem of college men getting along with ambitious and well-trained college women in marriage. College men need to grow up and accept women as equals and expect as much of their wives in the way of accomplishments as of themselves—not only expect it, but what is more important, accept it. This is a very hard thing for most men to do.

Richard Newberger, author and journalist of Portland, Oregon, is also a member of the state legislature. His wife was elected to the same legislative body. In a magazine article he has told of the time when he first accepted her as an equal and came to respect her as a person of real competence, rather than just as a wife, a companion, and the mother of his children.

An important bill was before the house and Mrs. Newberger was to speak on it. He confesses taking her aside and coaching her carefully in what to say. She was new in the legislature; he knew all the ropes, so he thought in the typical masculine manner. His wife thanked him generously, but having a mind of her own and ideas of her own, she went ahead and prepared her own talk. It was much more effective than the attack he had planned and he had to admit it, even to himself. He no longer regarded her with tolerance as sort of a second best in the marriage.

College men should quit kidding themselves and grow up enough to recognize that women are their equals, and college women generally just a little bit their superiors. (This is because a more select group of women than men go to college.) Those who are able to accept this fact can marry a wife who will be an asset to them, rather than try to revert to infancy and find a girl who will be another mother to them.

Girls need to get over the feeling that the marriage-versus-career dilemma is a major problem. With understanding on the part of the husband and adequate cooperation within the family, it is increasingly possible for the professional woman to have a career and marriage together. Children must have affection and care, but this does not mean that the able and talented mother must spend all her time with the children. With help in the home she often can carry on her career with only short interruptions. Moreover, she can often start her career before marriage, have it during marriage before children come, and with the increased length of life, continue it after the children are in high school, even if she drops out completely during the period when the children are small. The small family of today, say two or three children, if they are born close together, take up only about twenty years of the mother's life. This is a short span in the lifetime of seventy years, which women live today.

Marry now or wait? It is unfortunate that our society does not as yet subsidize college marriages in some way so that a greater number of able young men and women can marry and begin their families during college. In this respect the GI program for college training of veterans is unique. And it has been successful, in spite of the fact that many thought these men would be too rusty or too burdened with family matters to do well in college. They did well in college and increased the birth rate of the educated group, thus adding to both the competence of this generation and to the genetic qualities of the next.

As long as we do not subsidize college marriages generally, many young people face the difficult decision of whether to marry before finishing college. The problem is in part economic, although not entirely so. If the girl thinks she must have a career, then the answer is usually *no*. If she does not, she should not be too much influenced by her parents' or others' wishes that she get a degree for its own sake.

Ruth Read, in her book *Single Woman*, tells of older single women she interviewed who wished they had married in college when they had the chance. Instead, they passed marriage up because they or their parents wanted them to have college degrees. They ended up missing what most women must have in life to be happy—marriage and a family.

There are, of course, others who choose to delay marriage and in the end realize a better marriage than had they rushed into one. And there are certain to be a few who delay marriage and find ample satisfaction in a career.

The outcome is largely a matter of the young woman's values and aspirations. I have known successfully married college-trained women who were frustrated throughout their lives because children came early and they always felt they had missed the chance of making something of themselves vocationally. Studies of married women working or not working, too, show that it is what the woman wants that determines the effect of work on the marriage.

Those who want to work and can't are unhappy. Those who don't want to and have to are unhappy.

On the other hand, I knew a Ph.D. who had been a successful counselor until her retirement. She delayed marriage for a career, then further put it off because she could not give up her career. She finally saw the man she could have married, marry and rear a family. About the time she retired, this man was widowed, but before they could marry, he died. She was hoping to help care for his seventeen-year-old son, but in a matter of months he was in college. She missed out on family life altogether. I asked her if she felt she had been as satisfied with her life as if she had married.

She did not answer directly but said, "I have known a great many professional women, very successful women, and have never known one who did not someday hope to marry. I doubt that any woman is fully satisfied short of marriage."

In our society of privilege, choice is the right of all. When and whom one marries is a choice recently given to women as well as men. Choice always requires weighing alternatives and taking the consequences of one's own decisions. In some ways it would be easier to have an uncle, kinsman, or professional matchmaker to do the deciding.

Courses in marriage offer many guides to wise choice. In brief, some of the most important of these facts that bear on when to marry are:

1. Research shows that marriage of girls under nineteen and of men under twenty-two are very risky. Maturity is

essential to marriage today. Immature persons can rarely succeed.

2. Marriage after brief periods of acquaintance are extremely risky; few of them bring success. As Henry Bowman, professor of family life education at Stevens College, has put it, "Most marriage failures are courtship failures." The breakup of numerous war marriages is explained in considerable part by young people rushing into marriage and learning afterward that they have married a stranger who has no likeness to the person they wanted in marriage.

3. Marriage success runs in families; so does failure. One divorce judge stated, "It sometimes looks to me like divorce is hereditary." It's not exactly that. Temperament and disposition, learning to be pleasant or constantly bickering are learned patterns. Some families have traits that lead their children to develop pleasant and friendly dispositions; others the opposite. College people have a right to expect good marriages. Those with unfavorable backgrounds should take more than an average number of courses in marriage, family, child training, and parenthood, and learn how to act to be successful family members. One need not live by family tradition and perpetuate a cycle of bickering and meanness. Such persons particularly need time to acquire maturity.

4. Similar backgrounds, values, moral standards, and aspirations are important to success. Some great romances can grow out of differences and the novelty of strangeness, but few successful marriages come from such romances. Marriage today is a companionship of equal partners shar-

ing every aspect of their lives. Once marriage was a *state;* now it is an *adjustment.* Persons adjust best to each other who have a similar past and who can plan a like future. It takes some time to learn what the other person's real background is.

Some persons can marry successfully in the teens. Most cannot. Those who feel the urge should be especially sure they know themselves and the other person very well indeed.

Preparation for parenthood

College requires no preparation for parenthood, yet no young person can be prepared for life without it. Preparation for parenthood is one of the most neglected aspects of training in this age. Both the college man and woman should take courses in child care and training. Both should observe a nursery school and learn how to handle and guide children.

Most young people in this day of small families have not had the experience of handling and caring for babies in their own homes. Unless they get some training for it, they will face many critical problems and needless worries the day they bring the first baby home from the hospital. There is no excuse for such ignorance. We prepare far too often for almost everything but this.

All research into the subject shows that childhood happiness is of lifelong importance. Those who have a happy childhood adjust well to society. They are the ones who make successful marriages later.

Much marriage failure today is due to the fact that couples do not agree on how the children should be handled and trained. Most often it is the husband who is to blame. The college girl observes the handling of children in nursery school and knows something about the most effective methods of discipline and training. The college man does not, and begins handling his children later as his parents handled him. We learn better ways of doing things only by going where they are taught. Men should take the initiative in learning about children. If they do not, the girl should insist that her fiancé take courses with her or at least spend a certain amount of time observing a nursery school.

During the years following the Second World War, I had large numbers of veterans in my classes. Many were married and some had children. I insisted that they all spend some time during the semester observing in the nursery school, preferably with their wives. They did, and rather than coming back sheepishly, feeling that they had done something unmanly and effeminate, they reported that it had been a valuable experience and one from which they had learned a great deal which they could practice in their own families.

It is very difficult in our culture for men to realize that parenthood is for the man as well as for the woman. College men must lead the way in improving the male role in this respect.

No influence in life is so lasting as that which one has on his children during their first few years. There is no time to learn right ways when one is faced with the problem. No asset is so great to a child as to be handled properly and trained well by parents during the first few years, nothing so disastrous as to be handled improperly or to be in an atmosphere where the emotional climate is wrong.

College is the time to learn. Society has a right to expect better family life from the college-trained.

CHAPTER XVI

What Should I Expect of College?

Not good teaching

Don't expect good teaching. We college profs are chosen for what we know, not how we teach. Our salaries are determined primarily by the scientific papers we deliver before our learned societies, by our publications in scientific journals, which only our clan can read, and by statistics-filled monographs with a vocabulary that only the elect can translate. Teaching for us is frequently a side line. Often we are paid, like the football player, for bringing fame to the university which employs us.

If one of us should turn out to be a good teacher or a good Joe, it's quite by accident. We expect you to sit up and take notice whether you can understand what we say or not. There are always the textbooks. You can stay in your room and read them, if that's easier. Of course, you may not be able to pass the examinations that way.

In grade and high school, teachers are taught to teach. They study teaching methods in teachers' colleges, have to prepare lesson plans for the supervisor to look over, and are required to go through a period of supervised practice teaching where their work is watched and criticized. College profs never study teaching methods. They have never had practice teaching. No one ever has walked into their classroom to watch and criticize them. You'll have to be very tolerant of them.

A meeting of the minds

Most profs are aware of the fact that many students, particularly freshmen, have some difficulty adjusting to the lecture system, taking good notes, and comprehending clearly. As a result, they are generally willing to give whatever extra time and help they can afford to the struggling but serious student. Profs may look cold and indifferent, but most of them are eager to do a good, easily comprehended job. They welcome student questions and constructive criticisms.

Will college affect my income?

You have probably learned already that college shrinks your income pretty fast. In spite of that, I have known many students who were happy getting less than their money's worth. In making most purchases, we look the article over and ask for the best we can get. In college, many students want the cheapest article they can buy— easy courses, snap tests, good-natured profs who require little work.

Of course, when a student asks where college is going to get him in dollars and cents, he is thinking of the years ahead. Is the sacrifice of our parents and the part-time work, skimping, and saving we go through worth it?

There have been many small studies over the years

which have shown that the college graduate earns more than others. It was not until the 1940 census that we had any nationwide study of the earnings of any large group of the American public. At that time the Census Bureau asked those who worked for wages and salaries two questions: (1) the amount of salary or wages earned during the preceding year (1939), and (2) whether they had more than $50 additional income (investments, rents, etc.) during the year. In 1946 they published a report which showed earnings by education.

There were approximately 17.5 million male wage and salary workers whose only income was from salary or wages (less than $50 from other sources). This group is a fair test of the actual earnings of the college man compared with those of less education who are also on salary or wages.

Using these figures, I have made several comparisons. As you study them, you will see that the evidence proves conclusively that college pays in actual dollars-and-cents earnings. The college man earns more per year, he climbs longer during his lifetime in earnings, and his total lifetime earnings are far higher than those with less education.

These data are for a time when income was about half what it is now. Multiply all these figures by two, and you will have about what you may expect to earn, barring inflation or deflation of the dollar.

These figures are for men only. What about women? Does college pay in dollars and cents for them? The census gives us no answer, but sample studies do.

Time magazine studied 9,064 graduates from 1,037

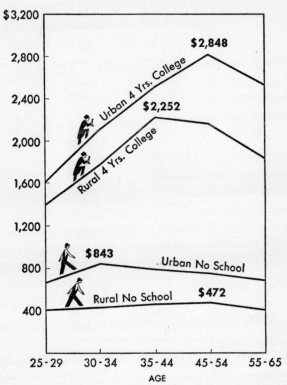

College boosts one up the economic ladder. Data are for male white wage and salary workers in the United States for the year 1939. Note that the earning peak is higher and the climb longer for those with more education. (Paul H. Landis, "The Dollar Value of an Education," Journal of the National Education Association, *38:366–368, May, 1949.)*

	Grade School	High School	College
		WHITE	
Total lifetime earning	$45,225	$66,745	$93,215
Average yearly earning	$1,131	$1,669	$2,330
		NEGRO	
Total lifetime earning	$27,025	$32,745	$44,020
Average yearly earning	$676	$819	$1,101

Average yearly and lifetime earning for white male wage and salary workers by education at 1939 levels. At present earning levels, amounts are twice as great. (Paul H. Landis, *"The Dollar Value of an Education,"* Journal of the National Education Association, *38:366–368, May, 1949.*)

American colleges and universities.[1] It was found that the college man climbs in income until he reaches fifty years of age and that 23 per cent reach or exceed $7,500 income per year. Only 1 per cent of women graduates reach this level. Of the men, another 22 per cent fell in the $5,000 to $7,500 earning group, but only 3 per cent of the women. Almost two-thirds of college women were earning less than $3,000. Only 14 per cent of men earned so little.

The world of earning still has a double standard. But granting that, do college women earn more than their sisters who do not go on to school? Our study [2] of over 3,000 young people in the state of Washington shows that the college woman greatly exceeds her less educated sisters in earning, even though she falls far below her male competitors. So even for the woman, college pays in spite of a discriminatory wage scale.

Will it affect my prestige?

Ah, to be somebody! Sweet thought. How much we struggle to occupy pedestals in the social system. Will that college degree help?

The *Time* study showed that in America over a third of college men are proprietors, managers, and executives; only 13 per cent of noncollege men are. These are the positions with swivel chairs and telephones at the elbow

[1] This study is presented in book form by Ernest Havemann and Patricia Salter West, in *They Went to College,* Harcourt, Brace and Company, Inc., New York, 1952.

[2] Paul H. Landis, "The Territorial and Occupational Mobility of Washington Youth," *Washington Agricultural Experiment Station Bulletin* 449, Pullman, Wash., July, 1944.

and which carry the responsibility of making decisions for others as well as oneself. They require directing the work of others and the management of both people and money. They are high-prestige positions.

The other high-prestige field in our society is the professions. The *Time* study showed that half of the college men enter the professions; only 3 per cent of noncollege men do.

In comparing the various professions with regard to income—and income is certainly one factor in prestige today—*Time* found that doctors were at the top in professional income, with lawyers second and dentists third. Of the doctors, 57 per cent earned $7,500 a year and over. In business, the best-paying field for the male graduate is banking.

Now let's look at the career woman. She fares poorly in pay, as we have seen, but not in prestige jobs. Of women graduates, 12 per cent are proprietors, managers, or executives, and 70 per cent are in the professions. The college woman does not lack fame, even if she does fall short of fortune.

At home in more social climates

The first-semester rhetoric book used in the author's college days had an essay on the "college-bred." It told how college men and women were at home in many more social circles than others. They knew more customs, had a richer vocabulary, were more tolerant of differences. They breathed an atmosphere of greater freedom than those who had not been within the doors of an institution of higher learning.

This is one of the greatest benefits of education. Business recognizes this in hiring executives. The government recognizes it in selecting many of its civil service employees.

There are many places in life where one is awkward without the college experience. This can be observed among the wives of college professors—all professors do not marry college women. The professor's wife who lacks a degree cannot be a member of the American Association of University Women. She feels awkward in many situations because she assumes that the college woman has something she lacks. She just never quite feels at home. There are, no doubt, many other occupations where this is true.

The author worked closely with a college president once. When we were traveling together one day, he confided, "I've never felt at home around a Ph.D."

"Why?" I asked in surprise.

"It's just one of those things I lack, and I can never quite relax because of it."

He had been a college president for years, presiding over a staff largely composed of Ph.D.'s, most of whom respected him and conformed to his institutional policies, yet he felt inferior because he terminated his education at the master's level.

In many situations a college degree is like that. It may seem very unimportant to one who has it, but the fellow without it thinks that he has missed something very im-

portant, that there are secrets in the college life which he
has missed out on.

Even in the most intimate kind of social relationships,
college helps. College marriages turn out better than marriages of noncollege people. College people, more than
others, stay married.

In one respect the college woman does not make the
grade socially as well as her untutored competitors. Although more college men than others marry, fewer college

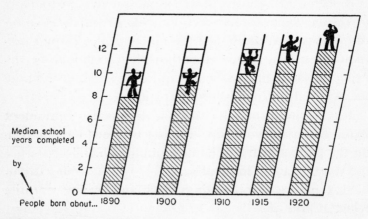

*Where will your generation be on the educational ladder? An
answer to this question determines the education you will
need to compete successfully. (Midcentury White House Con-
ference on Children and Youth.)*

women do. The *Time* study showed that at all ages more
college than noncollege women failed to marry. In some
cases this is a choice of a career and loyalty to a career in

preference to marriage. In such cases it is not always a failure in attracting a mate but a decision to remain single.

This situation is changing rapidly. In the early days of coeducation, very few college women planned to marry and few more than half did. Now most college women hope to marry and many plan to combine both marriage and a career.

It's the gateway to many lives

A degree is in some ways like money—there are so many places today where one can't go without it. It faces us on the job application. It faces us as a sort of informal prerequisite to many social situations. It has come to be the expected thing among those who exercise influence in the social system and who manage the affairs of men.

It is the most important way to a position of influence in our day and generation. Few dare to speak in the pulpit, on the political-party platform, in the halls of legislature or Congress, for business, the Army, or education without having first acquired the sheepskin, with the training which it presupposes. We had better be on our way!

Service

We who are privileged to acquire a college education—most of it at the cost of society—have a great debt to our fellowmen. It is our part to acquire a knowledge of the way in which we may serve, on a greater scale than we could without college, the interests and welfare of our time and generation.

The world is waiting to be remade by each new generation. There will always be the challenge to leave the world a better and happier place for our having lived and worked there.

It is this expectation that provides the leaders in all generations with a challenge and motivation that result in greatness.

Index

Date Due